EARLE BIRNEY

by Richard H. Robillard

Canadian Writers Number 9
New Canadian Library

McClelland and Stewart Limited
Toronto/Montreal

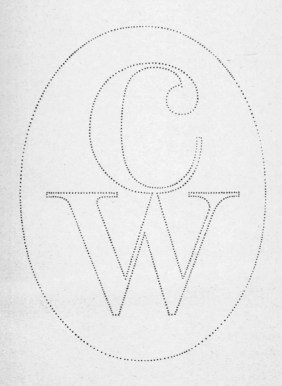

CANADIAN WRITERS

A SUBSERIES
IN THE NEW CANADIAN LIBRARY

Canadian Writers is a series of handbooks
designed to provide the student and general
reader with compact and inexpensive
introductions to significant figures on the
Canadian literary scene. Each book is
written expressly for the series by an
outstanding Canadian critic or scholar and
provides, besides a comprehensive critical
approach to a given author, useful
biographical and bibliographical
information.

NEW CANADIAN LIBRARY
Malcolm Ross, Editor-in-Chief

CANADIAN WRITERS
W. David Godfrey, Editor

© 1971 by McClelland and Stewart Limited

The Canadian Publishers
McClelland and Stewart Limited
25 Hollinger Road, Toronto 374

CONTENTS

Acknowledgements

I wish to thank the Ryerson Press for permission to quote from Birney's first three volumes, from his edition *Twentieth Century Canadian Poetry*, and from Desmond Pacey's *Ten Canadian Poets*. My thanks also go to CBC Publications for permission to quote from Birney's *The Creative Writer*. My special thanks to Dave Godfrey, the most helpful editor a writer could hope to have. I am indebted to Earle Birney for his comments and for permitting me to quote early poems and early versions of poems. SP indicates *Selected Poems*; ICBoS indicates *Ice Cod Bell or Stone*.

Dedication

To my
Mother and Father

General Editor's Note

This series was not designed to be definitive; what is eventually needed is at least thirty full-length studies of major Canadian Writers in English, but the task of even a preliminary survey is especially difficult with writers as prolific and complex as Earle Birney, working in different forms and constantly moving onward, before the critics have had time to properly analyse and assess the previous work. In his case then, it was decided to concentrate upon the earlier, more traditional poems, subjecting them to that meticulous *explication de texte* which they have long deserved. It is hoped that this process will help the reader work out his own interpretation of the important long poems *Once High Upon a Hill* and *November Walk Near False Creek Mouth* as well as the verse-play, *Damnation of Vancouver*, but no attempt is made in this text to deal with the two novels, *Turvey: A Military Picareque* and *Down the Long Table*, with his Chaucerian essays, his radio and TV writings, his short stories, or with the two books of new poems from the late sixties: *Pnomes Jukollages & Other Stunzas*, (1969), and *Rag & Bone Shop*, (1971). It would definitely be to the reader's advantage to have a copy of *Selected Poems, 1940-1966* at his elbow while working through this study.

INTRODUCTION

Alfred Earle Birney has no biographer, although the main outline of his public career has been drawn several times. For the
present, one can only guess at the specifically autobiographical
content of his novels, and one would like to know much more
about his reading. The following outline may at least suggest
something about the poet in the poem, and something of the
variety of his experiences.

Born in 1904, Birney spent his youth in Calgary, Banff, and
Creston, British Columbia, in the southern region of the
Kootenays. Of his parents, Birney has written:

> My parents were largely self-educated; my mother came
> from generations of Shetland fisherfolk and crofters; an
> immigrant girl, she was working as a waitress in a miner's
> hotel in the Kootenays when she married my father, who
> was the son of a small-town butcher. My father was by
> turns a cow-puncher, brakeman, prospector, paper-hanger,
> soldier, and unsuccessful bush-farmer.[1]

In Birney's novel *Down the Long Table* (1955), the father of
Gordon Saunders seems to bear some resemblance to Birney's
own father, and Gordon's boyhood jobs were also Birney's.
After his graduation from Creston High School in 1920, Birney worked for two years to earn money for university. In
"David" the kinesthetic imagery and the descriptions of the
work done by David and Bob – cutting trails on the survey, in
air that was steeped in the wail of mosquitoes – drew on Birney's youthful labour.

> . . . I was doing heavy farm work with horses before I was
> twelve; at sixteen, axeman; seventeen, swinging picks and
> sledgehammers on winter relief; eighteen, oiling swamps
> with a forty-pound barrel pump on my back. Eventually I
> paid my college fees from such work and from earned
> scholarships.[2]

At the University of British Columbia, Birney did indeed earn
several scholarships and prizes, as well as earning money as a
journalist, house-painter, and door-to-door salesman. Keeping
up his jobs and his grades, he somehow managed to find the
time, during his senior year, to edit the undergraduate newspa-

per, *Ubyssey*, and to write several poems for that paper. Birney graduated in 1926 with first-class honours in English literature.

In that autumn he entered the University of Toronto as a Leonard Graduate Fellow, and began to concentrate his studies on Old and Middle English; that growing interest bore fruit in his later imitations of the Anglo-Saxon verse-line, as in "Anglosaxon Street." He took his M.A. in 1927.

"From then on until World War II," Birney has written, "I . . . earned a lousy living as an academic, in between depression layoffs."[3] During the next seven years, 1927 to 1934, he studied at the Universities of California and Toronto, and taught English at the University of Utah and in the University of British Columbia Summer School. In 1934, he went to the University of London to spend a year doing research on Chaucer, and two years later he took his Ph.D. at the University of Toronto. His thesis is entitled "Chaucer's Irony." During the next six years, he taught at University College, the University of Toronto. Most of the *David* poems were written in that period. Birney was married in 1937.

He very ably served as literary editor of *The Canadian Forum* between 1936 and 1940, and wrote many book reviews for that journal. Some of those reviews and essays quite clearly indicate Birney's socialism in those years. He was to write later: "I was so all-fired clear-cut political in the Thirties I regarded the writing of poetry as a treacherous withdrawal of energy from the class struggle."[4] *Down the Long Table*, while not as good as *Turvey*, transforms the dreary teaching and the politics of the 1930's into a readable novel. With few exceptions, Birney's poems are not specifically about politics.

1936 to 1942 were busy, productive years, concluded by the appearance of *David and Other Poems* and by Birney's enlistment into the Canadian Army. During the last two years of the war he served in Europe and became major-in-charge of Personnel Selection for the Canadian Army in the North-West Theatre. The red tape and confusion of "selecting personnel" became the circumstances surrounding *Turvey*, the hero of the novel published in 1949; in it Birney comically exorcized some of his military ghosts who had hexed themselves with administering I.Q. and aptitude tests. Returning home, Birney became Supervisor of the Central European Section of the CBC International services,[5] and in the next year he took a position as Professor of English at the University of British Columbia. *Now Is Time* appeared in 1945. Between 1946 and 1948, he served as editor of *The Canadian Poetry Magazine*,[6] and in 1948 published *The*

Strait of Anian, a volume of poems.

He published his fourth book of poems in 1952: *Trial of a City and Other Verse*. The next year began the travels which were to be re-created in his poems. He spent much of 1953 in France, writing *Down the Long Table*.[7] In 1955 and 1956 he travelled in Mexico;[8] in 1958, to Hawaii, Japan, Hong Kong, Thailand, and India. During the 1958-59 academic year, as a Nuffield Foundation Fellow, he was in London, doing research on Chaucer's poetry. In Latin America and the West Indies in 1962 and 1963, as a Canada Council Senior Arts Fellow, he lectured on contemporary Canadian poetry. (In 1953 he had edited and published an anthology, *Twentieth Century Canadian Poetry*.) He also traveled in Europe in 1963.

Between 1962 and 1966, he published three books of poems· *Ice Cod Bell or Stone* (1962), *Near False Creek Mouth* (1964), and *Selected Poems, 1940-1966*. In 1962 he edited, with the assistance of Margerie Lowry, *Selected Poems of Malcolm Lowry*.[9] During the last months of 1965, he gave a series of half-hour talks on CBC; they were published the following year under the title *The Creative Writer*.

In 1963 Birney had become Chairman of the Department of Creative Writing at the University of British Columbia, and also editor of *Prism International*. As Writer-in-Residence, he served at the University of Toronto from 1965 to 1967, and then for several months at the University of Waterloo. In 1968 he was Regents Professor at the University of California in Irvine. In July of that year, as a Canada Council Fellow, he started on a year's trip to Australia and New Zealand, and to parts of the United States and Canada.

—Working in the out-of-doors, studying literature, teaching, editing journals, witnessing war, and travelling in Canada and in foreign countries: these are some of the activities which have informed Birney's poetry. One could speculate that his editing developed in him the habit of using his blue pencil on his poems, that studying the forms of Chaucer's irony sharpened the irony in his own poetry, and that his reading of the narratives in Old English literature led to his appreciation of epic and heroic poetry. The formal studies of this poet from the western mountains well equipped him to represent the collision of war and nature in his early poems.

Birney's poetry dramatizes and meditates on the relationships between the human and the inhuman. As I will suggest later, "Dusk on the Bay" and "Vancouver Lights," two early poems, offer complementary, if not opposing, attitudes toward nature and society. In the former poem, nature is seen to have a purposeful order, whereas man's order is arbitrary and sterile. In "Vancouver Lights," however, nature is black chaos, and man is Prometheus the light-giver. If these two poems are complementary, as I believe they are, there is implied a need for man to respect nature's processes, and, at the same time, a need for heroic struggle against the lack of human reference in nature.

On the axis of these poems rest a great many poems. In tone and theme, they range from the comic resignations of man to nature's ways ("Holiday in the Foothills") to the pathetic and terrible absorption of man by nature's forces ("Bushed"); from Birney's contrast between warring men and a purposeful nature to man's dehumanizations of himself by his despoilings of nature. Clearly, these tensions suggest that, although Birney is perhaps a romantic at heart, he is quite aware that we are living in a post-romantic era in which "nature poetry" must be written anew. Nature is "pointless" without human reference. The rhetoric of "David" and other poems strongly challenges the romantic reader. The quest to see nature as somehow humanly significant – to see that nature and man share meanings, while seeing that nature holds its own dominion – is the largest of Birney's motives in his poems.

Birney does not, of course, direct any messages to philosophers; he creates symbolic and rhetorical structures. Yet there is a goal implied, especially in the travel-poems, and there perhaps achieved; it is what I have called (somewhat clumsily) the real-as-myth. In the living, actual incarnation of myth, in the dancing of spontaneous, traditional people, in the intersection of eternity and the dazzling instant, one can at least glimpse at myth, the resolution of the human and the inhuman. In these later poems Birney conjures meanings from living situations, and the ironical perspectives of the earlier poems fade before his need to become involved in a realized myth.

What emerges from a study of Birney poetry is an impression of an intelligent poet who is alive to the resources of language and of poetic structure. To study the forms of his poetry is to learn how the meanings are realized. I hope that I have prepared a case for a more thorough study of Birney's craftsmanship; his best poems will, I think, bear close analysis. That is my immediate purpose in the following pages.

RICHARD H. ROBILLARD
Université de Montréal
January, 1970

1. DAVID

David (SP,118)[10] opens with a spate of reverberating sounds and rhythms; one is caught up in the swinging metres and sound-effects, in the physical flow of the syllables. Comparing the suffocation and the human commotions under the camp tents with the sunny freedom of the mountains, Part I uses a more-or-less prosaic syntax; it is the versification which knits up the prose strands, shapes the lines and stanzas, and creates much of the mood.

> David and I that summer cut trails on the survey,
> All week in the valley for wages, in air that was steeped
> In the wail of mosquitoes, but over the sunalive week-ends
> We climbed, to get from the ruck of the camp, the surly
>
> Poker, the wrangling, the snoring under the fetid
> Tents, and because we had joy in our lengthening coltish
> Muscles, and mountains for David were made to see over,
> Stairs from the valleys and steps to the sun's retreats.

Birney uses a long pentameter line here. Ranging from 12 syllables (1.8) to 16 syllables (1.3), the lines emphasize the anapestic metre (xx/), which accounts for 23 of the 40 feet of Part I. And except for the initial trochaic foot (/x) in one line 1 and in the four lines of stanza 2, the other feet are all iambic (x/). The dominant rhythm, then, is a rising one – rising from one or two weak syllables to a strong stress.[11]

The statistics duly noted, we may say that this iambic-an-apestic cadence is quite apt here; it suspends the very motions and activities which the words themselves denote. Of course, we cannot claim that this metre "imitates" what is described, but in a sense, the quick passing over of the weak syllables to get to the strong stress sets up a mood that parallels the muscular mean-ings of the action described. The anapestic can be, one cannot fail to remember, a very light, tripping metre; but Birney has carefully broken up many of the anapests to slow down the ti-ti-DUM ♪♪♩ He uses what is sometimes called a "lyric" cae-sura, the pause which in this case comes between the weak syllables of an anapestic foot.

x c x   /
- er cut trails (1.1)

x c x   /
- ges in air (1.2)

x c x   /
- toes but o- (1.3)

x c x   /
- gling the snor- (1.6)

x c x   /
- leys and steps (1.8)

(The "epic" caesura, on the other hand, is placed between the metrical feet. For example, in 1.5;

/ x c x   /
"Poker, the wran-.") Found in fairly relaxed verse, the lyric caesura in these lines does not violate the ordinariness of the syntax; it is quite in keeping with the tone of Part I.

The stanzas themselves are gently shaped. In making up the end-rhymes (a b b a), Birney uses suspended rhymes and asso- nance. Thus *survey-surly* rhymes the initial syllables only; *steeped* and *week-end* share the same vowel; *fetid* and *retreats* repeat the $\bar{e}$ and the dentals (*t* and *d*). The end-rhymes are there to create a pattern, but the pattern calls just a little attention to itself. In addition, the lines themselves alternate between end- stops and run-ons. At the end of lines 1, 2, 3, and 7 the pause, however slight, is syntactical; it divides one modifier ("on the survey") from another ("All week"), or a modifier ("over the sunalive week-ends") from the subject and verb ("We climbed"). There is in these cases, then, a correspondence be- tween the line as a metrical unit and the line as a syntactical unit. On the other hand, in lines 4, 5, and 6, the last word is an adjective which modifes the first word of the next line. In this case, there is no correspondence between the metrical line and the syntactical line. This kind of mixing gives us the impression, once again, of a firm but gentle shaping. The stanzas as stanzas do not cry out, but rest quietly under the fate of meaning and mood.[12]

But within the line and groups of lines, there is nothing quiet about the syllables; Birney presses hard on patterns of allitera- tion and assonance. In Part I the consonants and vowels halloo and cry; thus, the *w*'s of lines 2 and 3, the *m*'s of line 7, and the *s*'s of line 8. Nevertheless, the ear perhaps mistakes a confused clamour of sounds in Part I, for it becomes apparent that the sound-effects are, more often than not, carefully patterned. The largest pattern attends to the single line and to the halves of a line. In line 8, for example, each noun ends with an *s*, and each half-line contains one or two initial *s*'s and one c̄:

$\overset{1}{S}$tairs from the valleys // and // $\overset{1}{s}$teps to the $\overset{1}{s}$uns's retreats.

The scheme is thus: 1, 2: 1, 1, 2. This design of the sound-effects is far from being a formality, for it reinforces the very rhythm of the line. A larger but similar pattern is in line 2, which alliterates the *w*'s as well as repeating the c̄ of "valley" and "steeped." An interesting variation appears in the sound-crossing (chiasmus) of 1.3:

In the $\overset{1}{w}$ail of mosquit$\overset{2}{o}$es, but $\overset{2}{o}$ver the sunalive $\overset{1}{w}$eek-ends.

In the first half, the *w* precedes the *o*; but in the second half-line, this sequence is reversed – "over" precedes "week."

Of course, many of the effects in Part I resist schematic description; "the ruck of the camp, the surley/Poker, the wrangling, the snoring under the fetid/Tents" is a wonderfully evocative listing of noises. Nevertheless, one senses what Birney draws on here; words which suggest something of their meaning in their sounds. This phenomenon, called "phonestheme" or "phonetic intensive," implies a certain kind of sound-symbolism. For example, the *sn* of Birney's word "snoring" also begins a great many words with unpleasant connotations – "snivel," "sneeze," "snarl," and "snicker" come to mind; thus, Birney's word evokes some of the connotations within this phonic family of words. One could easily overstate the power and precision of phonesthemic words in a poem, and one could argue that "snow," for example, is not necessarily an unpleasant word. However, it is clear that phonesthemes exist in language, that the users of a language respond to them, and that poets draw on them. It was perhaps no accident that Faulkner gave the name "Snopes" to a clan of unwashed opportunists and schemers, and that Birney used "ruck," "wrangling," and "snoring" to describe the noises in the camp.†

† Mr. Birney writes: "'Ruck' is defined by Webster's as 'the crowd of ordinary persons or things'; it is not a word describing a noise." I thank Mr. Birney for looking up the word for me, and I agree that this is the primary meaning of "ruck"; but Mr. Birney will perhaps forgive me if I hear "ruck" as elliptical for "ruckus," which is indeed a noise. Of course, if there were no others noises indicated in the immediate context of the poem, and if the kind of noise connoted by "ruckus" did not fit the context, then Mr. Birney would be quite correct about the sole meaning of "ruck."

Most of the acoustic designs which I have been describing are almost invisible parts in a moving narrative. Yet, as we move with that flow, we are aware that it is directed, that the scenery is not accidental, and that the parts relate to one another to offer a single experience. It would be a mistake to accept Birney's actual scenery in "David" as one accepts the scenery seen through a window of a fast train; and it simply will not do to evaluate the scenery in "David" as to whether or not it is truly western Canadian scenery. To delight in the massive way in which Birney has represented the Canadian out-of-doors is, no doubt, a valid pleasure (although it is too often automatically associated with the delights of the city-dweller come on a distant mountain prospect). But to talk about such matters exclusively is to fail to discuss the *poetic ordering* of the landscape. Like Wallace Stevens' jar which tamed the wilderness of Tennessee, Birney's craft allows us to see a Canadian wilderness as humanly significant.

That significance lies very much in the ironies of Part I. During the weekdays, David and the narrator worked as aids to surveyors in the mosquito-infested valley. (Note that the alliteration of *week-wages-wail* identifies the time with the action – working for hire – and with the scene – the mosquito-infested valley.) The avocation of the two young men was to climb mountains during weekends. That contrast puts the matter of Part I in the plainest terms, and yet it loses the central issue of these lines. They pose the questions: What is truly *human* activity? How may one become human? That these are merely expedient ways of describing what Part I is "about" suggests the richness of Birney's lines.

One of many points of reference is, once again, lines 4-5. Birney has abstracted the life of the camp into the unpleasant noises of men and of mosquitoes. Furthermore, it is noteworthy that we do not see the men who make the noises; instead, we hear about "the wrangling," "the snoring," "the ruck." Nor do we hear about "surly poker-players," but about "the surly poker." Birney has used a metonomy: the name-of-the-game for the players-of-the-game. In keeping with the names for the other noises, this metonomy is quite suggestive: "*the* surly poker" quite definitely indicates that *whenever* poker was played, the players were *invariably* surly. The point is that, in the valley, the human is limited to making noises, to hearing the wail of mosquitoes, and to utility.

The irony which lines 6-8 bring to bear suggests that although the valley traditionally connotes security, "human" fellowship, rich bottom-land, etc., the human is not to be found there but rather up in the mountains, and, that although the weekend is traditionally a time for hobbies, relaxation, and household chores, the human act is performed then, performed in the world of nature rather than within human society. In Part I, ironies are pointed not by Birney's having chosen the most accurate words, but by his having chosen words for their ironic contrasts.

"Mountains for David were made to see over": the operative word here is "see." Unlike Hilary's wish to conquer a mountain because it is "there," David's desire is to see things which the mountains hide. An important qualification is implicit in line 8: "the sun's retreats." Here the mountains do not bar vision so much as their heights offer places of meditation and self-knowledge. By conventional standards, perhaps, the valley is the place of retreat – retreat from the sun; but that retreat is noisy and dehumanizing. Clearly, Birney contrasts the burley *sounds* of the valley with the *sights* achieved on mountain-tops, with visions which are, as "retreats" indicates, deeply felt as human and, even, religious. Birney's irony is actually couched in the language of paradox.

The mountains are "seen" in other ways as well. The joyous boys climb them *because* of "lengthening coltish/Muscles." There is indicated here an almost *necessary* connection between their high animal spirits and their avocation – the one is the cause of the other. In contrast with the auditory and olfactory images of the "fetid" camp, we have now a kinesthetic image – one of those which refer to muscular feelings of relaxation or tension. The irony here is that the human vision is reached by means of animal vitality. Finally, the metaphors of line 8 show us again the ironic way in which the mountains are viewed: they are "stairs" and "steps." These metaphors seem conventional pieces of fancy only to the reader who has failed to see that Part I is a radical questioning of "the human." The case-in-point is that David sees no separation between natural things and human artifacts (stairs and steps). The naif teleology in line 7 – mountains were made so that humans could see over them – has the same import: the mountains are at once both barriers and staircases.

"David" is about knowledge hard won, an initiation to the ironies of reality. It is perhaps fitting that the first assault should have been on "Mount Gleam," for "gleam" denotes a faint flashing of light, usually reflected light. In Part II one sees "the hurrying slant of the sunset," the "floating of mists," the glittering prairie, the "darkening firs," and shadows. The most striking image is "snow like fire in the sunlight" (1.9). In this paradoxical simile is nucleated a wealth of meaning, for in the world above the timberline is a light like no other, a light in which cold and heat are one. And, naturally enough, the knowledge is "won" (1.8) by the perspective. Seen from the peak, "the alien prairie glittered." Both prairie and valley, the places of man, are ephemeral and alien to the men of the mountains. Perspective also counts for losing "the lure of the faceted/Cone in the swell of its sprawling shoulders"; the gleaming cone is lost when the hikers near the mountain and are under its shoulders.

The mountain has shoulders, and its "peak was upthrust/Like a fist." Again, as in Part I, the mountain is humanized. In itself, the personification is conventional enough; and yet within the action of the poem, the hiking and climbing, something ominous is suggested. The fistlike peak thrusts up from a "frozen ocean of rock" that, though inert, frozen, "swirled into valleys." The fist is perhaps like that of a drowning swimmer. Whatever the case, the paradox of a swirling, frozen ocean is quite in keeping with the feeling so far.

As these ironies expand in the poem, they render the complex state of Bob's thoughts and feelings. Moreover, they are ways of articulating Bob's attempts to seize David's vision of man and nature. For David, the laws of man and those of nature are parallel, if not identical; and it is man's truly human purpose to realize that truth. David's vision is itself not paradoxical, but to Bob, the initiate, the pupil, nature is suffused with paradox. Several episodes in the poem represent David as Bob's tutor, and they specify the lessons.

The teacher himself – his ethos – is only implicit at first, but becomes increasingly apparent. In Part II David showed Bob "How to use the give of shale for giant incredible/Strides." The muscular kinesthesia of the imagery here suits that of the section and of the whole poem; but more relevant to the meaning is that this knowledge enables Bob to escape a danger: Bob jumps "a long green surf of juniper" and lands softly in gentian and saxifrage. (The etymological meaning of "saxifrage" – "rock-breaker" – might be kept in mind.) If we recall the other water and ocean images in Part II, "surf" again represents a danger to be overcome. David has provided the means.

At the end of Part II the water "knifed down a fern-hidden/Cliff." Once again, a conventional metaphor, even a cliché – just as facile as "the light knifed through the darkness." But the image is made precise by the context. The water is, one notes, "unseen" as it splashes in the shadows, and we recall that the whole of Part II is filled with a glimmering, shadowy light. Hearing apprizes one of things which seeing cannot know. Early in Part III the knife-image is repeated. Clinging on a "knife-edge," David and Bob pass the time "with the guessing of fragments/Remembered from poets, the naming of strata beside one,/And matching of stories from schooldays." Now seen and felt, the knife can be avoided by the human.

Fatefully, David spies the Finger on Sawback – an "un-mapped" spire. Is it suggested here that names cannot help one? The naming of strata can while away time, but this spire has only the name David gave it; it is unknown, and thus will be David's real test.

But before the climbing of Sawback, three episodes intervene (in Parts III, IV, and V); in them Birney has carefully anticipated the climatic episode, the death of David. The skeleton of the mountain goat, its ribs splayed on a rock (Part III), is repeated in the image of the mangled David, "his legs/splayed beneath him"; and David's killing the wounded robin (Part V) anticipates Bob's "killing" his wounded friend. Even a mountain goat – even the naturally skilled – can slip and die, Bob learns, and his simple kindness is challenged by David's appeal to a hard truth – the code he lives by. This code is never fully grasped by Bob, whose own knowledge is implicit in the ironies and paradoxes of the whole poem.

We can now say that to the initiate, Bob, the mountain and the life of mountain creatures are infused with paradox, for he cannot see them as they are, as "natural," but only as they may be explained, or accommodated, by his comparing them with things outside the world of the mountains. That, I take it, is the rationale for the central images: they represent a state of mind, that of the narrator, which is only slowly becoming aware of David's code. Thus, from a more-or-less rhetorical point of view, the narrator stands between David and us, the readers – or at least those readers for whom mountains are mountains, and people people. The contrary, as we said in discussing Part I, is true of David's view, for his code makes no distinction between wounded robins and wounded men. When one's very *anima* – that which distinguishes one, and makes for the kind of life one lives – is wounded, physical death is preferable to spiritual death.

The two episodes in Parts III and V are no more important than the one in Part IV; without it David's code and death could be considered to be merely romantic and even perhaps adolescent. A surgeon whose hands are mangled in an accident should not ask his colleague to kill him, we say. And a man lives so that other men can live, we say. But David's point of view is different, for a death is not necessarily entombed and thus shut away from understanding, from knowledge, but may be communicated, represented. This is the import of the second stanza: David teaches Bob to read "the beetle-seal [the seal of death] in the shale of ghostly trilobites,/Letters delivered to man from the Cambrian waves." Furthermore, I suggest that now that we have been reminded of the fact that the land was once covered by water, we can now put into perspective the "ocean" and "surf" images in the poem. In Part II the "frozen ocean of rock" was just a metaphor; however accurately it represented Bob's feelings, it was an importation of something foreign into the scene. But now, at least in retrospect, we can see that the ocean of rock is not a mere metaphor but a fusion of past (Cambrian) and present; it is a symbol of nature's violence. The point is, once again, that Bob's paradox of a frozen, swirling ocean of rock suggests a knowledge of nature which subsumes both the literal and the metaphorical. Bob's is the language of symbol and paradox, and his poem is itself a "letter" about death.

After such revelations and portents, Part VI is a momentary anticlimax. That is its purpose, perhaps. It is an interlude, an idyll, and thus leads us a little off the main track, gives us a rest from knowledge. Here nature is very much alive, pulsing out rich scenery and providing food for man. Only the marten (the "scout" for the genius of the mountain?) is slightly ominous.

Quite appropriately, Part VII begins and ends with the "unknown"; David's endangering himself and his fall on the unmapped Finger are concluded by "the muted beat of unknowing cascades." If the submerged metaphor here is that of the funeral tattoo, the line is charged with irony, for the cascading water is ignorant of David's plight. This implication has the effect of qualifying any romantic assumption that nature is somehow attendant on man, that nature feels for man's suffering. And indeed, the rhetoric of the poem's ironies powerfully confronts the reader romantically inclined.

Up to Part VIII, the poem has pressed very lightly on the friendship of Bob and David; the narrator has offered no introspective, discursive accounts of his "thinking," or of his feeling toward David. Any drama implicit in the earlier episodes is resolved in descriptive narration. Those descriptions, often rendered in ironical terms, tell us a great deal about Bob's sensibili-

ty, but they do not let us know very much about his "character." To that end the last two sections of the poem turn, although they do not, finally, throw a piercing light into Bob's
ethics. Of course, the poem in no way judges Bob's "killing" of
David, except in rendering Bob's rationalizations. At any rate,
experience is opaque. Part VIII is a painful self-revelation.
Against it is Bob's "lie" (1. 24), for he knows that the hope
which he holds out to David is futile, and he knows that David
knows. David blames himself for the accident, but before Bob
pushes David over the ledge, Bob admits to himself that it was
he who had not tested his hold. There is, finally, no moral
cowardice in Bob.

Doubtless, a short story could heighten the moral drama of
Part VIII, but would have to do so in ways foreign to the
descriptive emphasis of the poem.[13] The paradoxes are sharp in
this section. David's eyes *brighten* with fever, and yet he does
not speak because of the"*clouding* fever." "In the sun it grew
cold." But the most important change is signalled by the nature
imagery. Perhaps the most telling image is in the penultimate
stanza: ". . . the last joint of the Finger/Beckoning bleakly the
wide indifferent sky." Nature herself (or itself) seems indifferent,
unknowing. At the beginning of Part VIII, Bob's call gets "no
answer but echoes/Released in the cirque." No longer a provi-
der for man, nature has stony fangs (1. 10) and thirsting lichens
(1.24) that drink David's blood. The vulture-like hawk (anticipated by Part III) and the waterfall, purring catlike, await David's death. In Part IX, running from Sawback, Bob projects his
shock and panic into nature. At best, nature is indifferent; the
clouds that linger over the ledge of the Finger are "incurious."
At worst, she is a grave, a canker, a fanged mouth.

The denouement runs counter to the theme of the poem; in
his shock, Bob cannot meditate on the "meaning" of David's
death, or on what I have called David's code. David himself was
not sentimental toward nature, but respected it as a being in
itself as well as a place in which man could discover and use his
humanity. Those correspondences which David saw between nature and man transcended the merely affective or romantic. In
the eyes of the dying David, he was the wounded bird that had
to give up its life. But Bob forgoes his education, and can only
see nature as frightful. The Bob of the last section anticipates
the crazed trapper in "Bushed," a later poem.[14]

2. MAN, NATURE, AND WAR

In Birney's first book, the title poem surveys the ground of most of the other poems. Granted that no other poem has a persona who quite resembles Bob, several poems have a narrative, or quasi-narrative, structure. Many of the poems ask how one may know nature, and the range of answers contains and limits the speculations about society. It is as though Birney had been groping toward a poetic comprehension of nature in order to frame a kind of pastoral world within which man, having distanced himself from society, might all the better understand society – and wars. This is the overt theme of "Hands" (SP, 75), "Holiday in the Foothills" (SP, 115), "Dusk on the Bay" (SP, 78), and "Kootenay Still-Life" (D, 22). Nature is the inexhaustible mine of analogies.

The analogies are sometimes facile, glib, poorly focused, and at times actually confused or sentimental. In "Eagle Island" (D, 23), the speaker, clapping heavy-handed ironies, compares the man-spoiled shores of Lake Ontario to the wild, tide-cleansed shores of British Columbia. The rhetoric of that poem, and of others like it, admits no self-questionings, no counter-ironies – there is little here of the complexity of "David." "Hands" is a case in point. Its radical contrast is between the "hands" of trees and those of civilized, warring men. Granted any situation, this contrast would still be hard to sustain convincingly, but one notes that the attempt is made. The speaker is drifting in a canoe "by the inlet's high shore" and musing on the "still green hands" of the trees bending to the water. He is bewildered, frustrated, made to feel alien by the "manumission" of the leaves. So far, and a few lines further on, a rich drama of reflection is implied, and the language itself is filled with nuances. In 1. 3, "still" is both adjective ("quiet") and adverb ("ever"). Silence and constancy are indeed deliberated in ironical terms. Now, as well as in the past (" the dead days of peace"), the liberating meaning of nature is too "bewildering." The notational pun "be-wild-ered" suggests the cause of his confusion: made wild by living in nature, he can no longer understand the folly of men. It is this state of mind which allows him to speak, paradoxically, of "the dead days of peace," for although men did not kill each other then, the past is "dead." And it allows him, musing on nature's cycle of decay nourishing new life, to speak of a noiseless battle for life, a "battle steeped in silence." Birney has also wittily punned on both meaning and situation. Thus "manumission" means liberation and puns on the Latin root "manus", "hand", the central image of the poem. Moreover, he has risked a fanciful play in l. 10: "My species would wither away from the radio's barkings." To "bark" a tree – to strip it of its bark – often results in killing the tree. And of course the image of a barking dog anticipates the next animal image of the chimpanzee. The ethical appeal of the speaker rests in his witty commentary on his frustration; and, as presented, his bewilderment is carefully controlled.

But the speaker soon turns rhetorician: there is no confusion in the rest of the poem, but a grinding amplification of the contrast between a purposive nature and a purposeless, mechanical, and brutal world of men. Thus, the cedar's hands are "Inept to clutch the parachute cord." The speaker stacks his deck often against mankind. He says that his own "fingers/ Must close on the paddle," that he must go "Back to the safe dead/Wood of the docks," but the personal intrusion here is left hanging, and the best that the rhetorician can do is to end on portentous pathos: "We are not of these woods, we are not of these woods,/Our roots are in autumn, and store for no spring."

(Commenting on "Hands" in his book *Ten Canadian Poets,* Desmond Pacy argues:

> It is not simply that nature is good and society bad. Nature is cruel as society is cruel – the cedars have webbed claws just as men have hands that fix bayonets and bombsights – but the cruelty of nature is part of a constructive pattern ("The fallen have use and fragrantly nourish the quick"), whereas that of society is purely destructive and arbitrary.[15]

The last is true enough, but it seems to me that Birney makes very little of nature's own cruelties. That the cedar has "claws" is the only wild card in his sharpster game against society.)

When humans populate these poems of *David,* more often than not they are seen as aliens or merely as litter-bugs. Certainly the speakers are not human-haters, but they do see men in the wilds as smaller than life-size and as a motley foreground – as in "West Vancouver Ferry" (D, 16). In "Grey Rocks" (D, 20), the "Lament of ukuleles," "the choke/And belching of a motor," and human "voices" wail/ing/Laconic time" counterpoint the "dark timeless pain" of the labouring tide. The arch tone obtrudes when the speaker describes the scene as a "saga," an ancient heroic story, which is in no way implicit in the choiring human voices.

Among the other poems which were not reprinted in the 1966 volume are "Reverse on the Coast Range" (D, 17) and "October in Utah" (D, 19). Less objective than "West Vancouver Ferry" and better focused in their imagery than is "Grey Rocks" these poems see the violence of nature in a way which immediately humanizes nature. This is the way of allegory and of emblematic poetry. In "Reverse on the Coast Range" the determining metaphor is warfare; the valley is assaulted by the flooding avalanche. There is no question here as to whether the "pathetic fallacy" of Ruskin's is fallacious, for allegory is based on correspondences of the following kind:

> Far away the dogwood heard and, clutching
> The dreams of their waxen vanities,
> Fled down the seaslopes.

Still, this is not the way of "David," nor of the better poems of Birney's first volume. In them, nature and man share meanings, but nature holds her own dominion and is therefore not wholly captured by allegorical metaphors.

Worth reprinting here is "Kootenay Still-Life." Its spirit, though not its form, is haiku: a small tableau in which images present a revelation apart from allegory.

Kootenay Still-Life

> Columning up from crisscross rot
> (Palmed flat by a wind forgotten)
> Breathes a single bullpine, naked
> For fifty cinnabar feet, then shakes
> At the valley a glittering fist of needles
> Rivergreen. And stops, headless.

> On the yellow fang of the bullpine's broken
> Neckbone sits, eyeing her mouse below,
> A crow.[16]

Granted the signs of humanity – "palmed," "fist," "neckbone" – the poem counters an allegorical reading with many ironies. It is a headless tree, though it "breathes" (which is botanically reasonable enough). And the "yellow fang" on the neckbone jabs into our emblematic eye. (Because the tree is headless, the neck is as good a place as any for the fang.) If we must take the image somewhat literally, then this piece of surrealism is at our expense and our risk. At any rate, this poem, like the haiku, is a poem of perspective. Looking from the "crisscross rot" up the naked trunk of the tree, seeing the needles falling, and stopping at the headless top, we finally and suddenly see the tree, not now grotesque and violent so much, as the place for the ancient watch of the crow for its victim. Coming upon the eyes of the crow, our eyes stop, and the poem ends. The poem is a "still-life" only in its last image.

A better Imagist exercise, "Smalltown Hotel" (D, 21) is more of one piece. (It was later revised and reprinted as "Decomposition," in SP, 115. The following is the text as it appeared in *David*.)

Smalltown Hotel

Cornered by two sprawling streets
The yellowed stiff hotel is stuck
A golden tooth within the buck-
Mouthed prairie town. Agape it greets
The evening's halfmoon sky. Within
The fly-loud dining-room a thin
Old waitress chants the bill-of-fare
To one bored traveller for kitchen-ware.

Every image counts. The hotel is "cornered" by life, as the hunted is cornered by the hunter; a useful ornament – a golden tooth – it is nevertheless a "yellowed stiff hotel." Are we to hear the echo of "scared stiff" here? Or are the two adjectives coordinate, in which case "yellowed" is simply descriptive of age, and "stiff" suggests lack of vitality and perhaps a stiff gentility? Are we to think of "yellow" as cowardly? "Buck-mouthed" is heard, but certainly the usual locution is "buck-toothed." But "buck," suggesting the masculine, anticipates the salesman in the dining room. The irony, perhaps, is that it is the hick, the rube, the Uncle Silas, who is popularly pictured as buck-mouthed, but at the end of the poem, the hick turns out to be the "bored" salesman – bored because he is in a hick town. That he should sell kitchen-ware is ironically fitting. In this masculine world, the one woman serves as dried-up priestess, chanting out the bill-of-fare. The poem is playfully suggestive. Its punning stems from two sources: first, its use of conventional locutions (such as I have described already), and, second, the situation itself and its focus on mouths and on eating. Thus if the mouth of this town is "agape," and if the hotel-tooth is in the mouth, then it is sure that this mouth will catch flies. If the traveller is "bored" by the hotel, a pun is realized because the hotel is a gnawer itself! The poem's humour rises out of the variations on the basic metaphor.

— "Dusk on the Bay" and "Vancouver Lights" (both reprinted in SP) are the most thoughtful of the war poems in *David,* or, at least, of those poems in which Birney meditates on war at some length. In these two poems, Birney's control of his attitudes toward war is masterful. Imagistic tableaux were easily painted by Birney; the meditative poem is a much more difficult creation.

The central symbols are light, heat, and the sun. In them, "Dusk on the Bay" (SP, 78) finds almost its total organization. In the first 20 lines the sun sets on English Bay. With its reek of hotdogs and chips, the scene is a little vulgar, but pleasant and familiar: a beach at dusk, dimly seen bathers, lights over the water, the moon above the lamps along the promenade. True, the scene is not altogether pleasant, for the sand is "foot-pocked," the bathers' legs "unsexed," their "waving arms severed with twilight," the divers are "quenched," the caustic night eats into the western sky. But the changes of colours in the sky are not, despite the metaphor, quite unpleasant, and people are at play. Besides, the scene repeats, in various guises, a principle of human order; light. In the opening lines, the key word is "perfect":

The .lighting rooms perfect a checkerboard across apartment boxes.

Lighting rather than lighted, the rooms compose a symmetrical order, and the theme of play is implicit in "checkerboard." And again Birney reins in what might have been too strong a theme by his ending the sentence with the slightly pejorative "apartment boxes." The lamps too compose a linear order (the "files" of lamps), albeit "regimented"; and even the cream arcs of the divers represent a man-made pattern. The heart-like beat of the lamps, "pulsing eveningly," suggests the human. Perhaps the one image which compares nature's order to man's is the following:

> The moon behind a row
> of moons along the promenade contracts and yellows
> upward

Nature, it would seem comes off second to man.

But man's order and man's light on this western Canadian shore are illusory; and to believe that nature's night, "this precious night," can ever catch tomorrow's sun is also illusory, for "tomorrow's sun is clean escaped." The sun which will flood the Canadian West tomorrow is already over Asia. The action, from line 20 to the end, follows the sun to the Atlantic shore of North America. The images in these lines counterpoint, in reverse order, those images of the first 20 lines. Thus, the Asian skies are garish with "unarrested rocket" (1. 22) whereas in lines 11 to 13, the evening star was "an arrested rocket." This early in the second half of the poem, therefore, the whole relationship between nature and man is reversed. Nature arrests her rocket; man's destructive rockets whizz on. Man's bombs make destructive "craters" (lines 23-24), whereas the craters of the moon do no damage. Man's gods are his guns, from which he pours out flaming "libations." The counterpointing goes on relentlessly. The blanching hulks of wrecked ships off Narvik (the town in northern Norway destroyed by Nazi bombers) repeat the "whitening ribs of the diving raft" in line 7. Now, "quenched" (1. 27) means drowned (compare lines 7-9). No longer do distance and dim light "unsex" the limbs of bathers; the limbs of war victims are "unsexed" because they have been blown off bodies (1. 29), and "the rain of iron" cools the flesh. No more the "reek" of popcorn, hotdogs, chips, but the stench of maimed flesh. And the light in apartment houses which had made a "perfect" checkerboard becomes in England the flame which "probes the tenement ruin" (1. 31), the flame "untamed" by man. (Note the distinction between the more expensive "apartment" and the cheaper "tenement.") Unlike man's light – utilitarian and "aesthetic" (here, creative of arbitrary, mechanical patterns) – nature's sun illuminates the failure of man to achieve order. The closing lines say as much – and more;

> Speeding and soaring he comes   the Atlantic
>   sighting
> and there is no Joshua can brake his flight nor
> any clutch of ours can hold this precious night

– precious because it fosters man's illusions. In the illumined face of war, no clutch of ours can hold on to our illusions, and there is no one to stop the sun from revealing war.

"Dusk on the Bay" is a very fine poem: deeply felt, fully articulated, and alive to deadly ironies.

The regimented lamps of that poem become, in "Vancouver Lights" (SP, 76), winking sparks of man's city in the vast darkness of space. In the "cosmos," which to the Greeks was synonymous with "order" and "harmony," man's world is his "dwarfdom"; and the night, the "velvet" chaos, "wraps ocean land air and mounting sucks at the stars." Thus, the three primal elements of water, earth, and air are annihilated, and even the fourth, fire (the stars), is threatened. Man is only a glowworm, a firefly, against the dark. He is also figured in the submerged metaphor of the spider, which "weaves . . . in gossamer"; the lighted city "webs the sable peninsula" (1. 4).

In the second verse paragraph, Vancouver is indicted; the speaker is both judge and defendant. Now, the lighted city – this domesticated "quilt of lamps" – is a "troubling delight" (an oxymoron which sums up the feeling of the poem thus far). War in other parts of the world brings the primal darkness "to this winking outpost." This section suggests the question: Can we, having lived through careless, thoughtless, spiritless years, read the message of the "primal ink"? The great irony is, of course, that there is little whiteness or brightness to set off the message: the ink floods almost the whole page. This implication is continued in the next verse paragraph, in which darkness is deified: "the stark ranges of nothing." More shockingly, the universal darkness is personified as the "black Experimentress" who looks at the universe on her microscope slide. Man's earth is a sub-microscopic particle which is beneath the scope of the gods. Even the sun, our Phoebus, "himself is a bubble that dries on her slide." This whimsical scientist will not trouble herself to discover the earth.

Yet, the defendant must speak up for men. We created our tiny sparks ourselves; we attempted to project ourselves and our order to the heavens. We are ourselves figured in the constellations. If man is extinguished, the Plutonian descendants of man must know that Prometheus, the light-giver to man, was his own torturer. ("Plutonian" ably suggests both the demonic underworld and the overworld of the planet Pluto.) The poem is finally addressed to other beings; and the communication is a poem, the most powerful and the most precise message of man's. The light in the last line is perhaps that of Genesis, and that of the gospel of St. John.

Yet the poem ends not with God's light but with man's. The image of man as demi-god, as Prometheus struggling against the darkness of nature, admits into Birney's poetry an understanding of the hero's attempt to create a human world, a world whose myths can establish man's place in nature and relate man to man. That large motive is dramatized again and again in Birney's volumes. It underlies, as I will suggest later, the major conflicts in the "Canadian" poems and in the poems about Birney's travels in foreign lands. Some of the travel-poems perhaps resolve those conflicts.

3. TWO ANGLO-SAXON POEMS

Trained in Old English poetry and language, Birney tried his hand at the alliterative line in such poems as "Anglosaxon Street" (SP, 80) and "War Winters" (SP, 82). In his Preface to the *Selected Poems*, Birney reproves the ignorance of "some teachers of Eng. Lit." who thought these two poems to be "defective imitations, fifty years too late, of Gerard Hopkins. In fact [continues Birney] they are adaptions of the alliterative modes and accentual patterns basic to English poetry about twelve centuries ago" – as indeed they are. (Some reviewers even thought them to be avant-garde!)

Anglo-Saxon meters and alliterative patterns are often very complex, but the essential form is simple enough; and we can use the first four lines of "Anglosaxon Street" as illustration.

Dawndrizzle ended   dampness steams from

blotching brick and   blank plasterwaste

Faded housepatterns   hoary and finicky

unfold stuttering   stick like a phonograph

Principally, one counts the number of primary stresses per line, not the number of syllables (which in these lines ranges from 8 syllables to 11). Thus, each line has 4 stresses, 2 in each hemistich (half-line). And all of the meters (except the first foot of line 4) are "falling" meters, either trochaic (/ x) or dactyllic (/xx). The feet themselves march to a very regular cadence, for there is nothing to stop the pulsating beat of the alliterated and stressed syllables. In 1. 3, we might hear

DUM-di DUM-di-di
Faded   housepatterns

DUM-di-di DUM-di-di
hoary and finicky

Metrically this is the case, but the temporal (musical) scansion of line 4 oversimplifies and actually distorts the actual rhythm and there is great rhythmic variety in just these opening four lines. "Patterns" is certainly slower than "-icky," even though the abstract scheme would identify them as equal in duration (here, as 16th notes); and "house" is longer than the initial syllable of "faded." The metre (the basic pattern of weak and strong syllables) fights the rhythm (which denotes, among other things, vowel-length, pitch, and the quality of consonants); and this tension constitutes the overall rhythm.

The patterns of alliterations strongly influence the rhythm. Lines 1 and 2, respectively, flood themselves with *d*'s and plosives (*b*'s and a *p*). In lines 2 and 3, the second hemistich reverses the order of the first alliterations: (1. 2) *f, h: h, f*; and (1.3) *f, s: s, f* (*f*onograph). A considerable number of variations – all of which affect the rhythm – can be wrought out of what seems to be a rigid design. The nature of the caesural pause also influences speed and, thus, rhythm. If the first hemistich ends with a syntactical or grammatical period, the line is truly halved; but if the syntax runs on to the second hemistich, the caesura is only metrical and, thus, relatively brief, as in

Imperial hearts   heave in the haven

And the groundrules for these variations are all implicit in Old English poetry.

But do we feel that this verse-form is somehow appropriate to the matter and tone of "Anglosaxon Street"? Of course, that the ancient WASP (White, Anglo-Saxon, Pagan) verse-form is used to describe modern WASP's is itself the signal for the ironies in the poem's matter, the major irony being that the moderns have no understanding of their history. A lower-class neighborhood (although the speaker is not himself "class-conscious" – he is no snob), its buildings decaying, its life monotonous and subject to

26   *Earle Birney*

blind prejudices against "nigger and kike," its rotting, greasy airs, its standardized patriotism and pleasures: all these are cast in the heroic mould of the verse-form which itself calls attention to the hum-drum of its content. Those reviewers who failed to see the verse as traditional failed to see its main irony.

"War Winters" is somewhat different. More symbolic than "Anglosaxon Street," and freer in its rhythms, "War Winters" uses the Old English verse-form to express a private vision of the war. Like "Anglosaxon Street," it uses "Germanic" compoundings and epithets – "heartcharmer," "hammerdent" (although the discrete words are not always themselves of Germanic origin). The Saxon diction and locutions well serve the ironic tone; they mime the whimsical yet real frustration of the speaker in war-time. The war winters and their snows transform the proud, beautiful sun into a chimneyplug, a sucked wafer, a dent on the hardiron sky. As in the other "Saxon" poem, the heroic becomes pathetic to alien eyes, to lodgers and to the visitor in a tenantless room. The sun gives no warmth; the fireplace is plugged, and the sacramental wafer is sucked dry. People are drowned in excremental snow ("dun droppings"), and they themselves are yoked as draft-animals are yoked. This last implication is set up by the epithet "peltwarmer" the sun warms the animal "pelts." The speaker seems wholly identified with the people of wartime. Even the epithet "proud Bessemer" attributes to the sun the name of the modern maker of steel. The obsessions of the age are implicit in its metaphors.

And yet, although all this is phenomenologically just, these impressions are not wholly caused by circumstances of time ("the months") and place ("latitude") Not that the metaphysical issues are wholly resolved – the poem is modest enough; but it does, I believe, transcend the wartime commonplace which 'says that the world is bad because the times, the time of war, are bad. The poem universalizes its situation, and sees all of earth's history and fate as sorrowful. It is, I think, a more profound poem than "Anglosaxon Street."

"War Winters" sounds different too. Its alliteration patterns are just as strident as those of "Anglosaxon Street," but its meters do not "fall" as regularly. True, a number of lines may be scanned to discover the trochees and dactyls that characterize the other poem. Line 9, for example:

chiefly the months   mould you heartcharmer

Or the three-footed line 13:

> /   x   \ | / \ | / \   x
> this your one wrynecked   woedealing

In the first stanza, the "greater iconic" foot (*//*xx) falls hard three times:

> /   / x x
> proud Bessemer

> /   /   x   x
> scan sky for you

> /   / x x
> white simpleton

But other lines mix or alternate falling and rising meters, or in a few cases use predominately rising meters. Line 4 is made of an anapest and three iambs:

> x   \   / | x   / | x   / | x   /
> The dun droppings blur   we drown in snow

Line 10 is iambic-anapestic except for the second foot:

> x   / | /   x   x | x   / | x x   /
> to scant hammerdent   on hardiron sky

(And we hear the ionic foot fall again in "scant hammerdent.")

If one objects that Anglo-Saxon verse had no "foot-prosody," that the Saxon poet merely counted the number of strong stresses (usually four) per line and let the weak syllables shift for themselves – if one maintains, therefore, that there are no "feet" in "War Winters" or in "Anglosaxon Street" – his objection is well taken. Nevertheless, he must somehow account for the rhythmic differences between the two halves of each of the following lines.

> x   \ | /   x | /   x   x | x x / | x   x   /
> (1. 5) Is this tarnished chimneyplug   in a tenantless room

> /   x   \ | / x x | x / | x   x   /
> (1. 11) not alone latitude   to lodgers on this

Footed or footless, the second hemistich of each line feels different from the first hemistich; there is a real tension between the two halves. And one may note that secondary stresses complicate the four thumping beats per line. The whole effect of the poem's versification is that it adapts the traditional Old English line, and that its freedom from the rigidities of that line creates something more than an imitation.[1]

4. NOW IS TIME: WAR, LOVE, AND SYMBOLS

In 1945 Birney published *Now Is Time*, a volume of war poetry. The first group of poems, "Tomorrow," speculates on the fatefulness of World War II – can peace be maintained? it asks. Group Two, "Yesterday," begins with poems representing the start of the war as seen from Canada: five of the six poems here are reprinted (with some changes) from the *David* volume, and are, indeed, among the best poems of that first book: "Hands," "Vancouver Lights," "Dusk on the Bay," "Anglosaxon Street," and "War Winter." This "Yesterday" group also prints thirteen poems dealing essentially with the war itself. The last group, "Today," represents the immediate aftermath of the war.

In *Now Is Time*, only a few poems rival the earlier "Dusk on the Bay" and "Vancouver Lights"; those few poems excepted, the war seemed to have stunned the act of meditation. In many, Birney often chooses imagery for its shock rather than for its wealth of suggestion. In "Dusk on the Bay" the images were grounded in a concrete situation, and they shared the closest intimacy. The rhetoric in *Now Is Time* offers sentiment of the common types, and that kind of brutal ugliness which is only the other side of the sentimental coin. Only a fine poem *as* poem will continue to shock its readers.

These speculations may explain such a piece of rhetoric as "Status Quo," the first poem in the volume; and they suggest why "Time Bomb" comes off rather well.

Time-Bomb

In this friend's face I know
    the grizzly still, and in the mirror;
lay my ear to the radio's conch
    and hear the atom's terror.

In each high stalk of wheat
    I watch osmotic rise of blood;
through nightsky see new firedrakes hosed
    with light and lead.

> Within the politician's ribs,
> within my own, the time-bombs tick.
> O man be swift to be mankind
> or let the grizzly take.[18]

The speaker meditates under high pressure; he recognizes the mirror-image of the brute not only in other men but in himself. The atom bomb will destroy mankind and allow the grizzly to "take" the world. Destruction immanent, the time-bomb set and ticking, nature is already transformed: the conch, with which we used to listen to the sea, becomes the radio announcing the terror of nuclear fission. In the second stanza (which Birney did not reprint in SP), nature is again transformed: the wheat is nourished by bloody ground; and in this apocalyptic vision, new Leviathans, the "firedrakes," are attacked by man's own destructive light (searchlights) and lead (gunshells).

And yet, the second stanza notwithstanding, there is much control, even understatement, in the poem. The terror is in what the speaker sees and hears, but he does not break up under that knowledge. He can even manage two oracular, sententious lines at the end of the poem. But although they are sententious in form and, apparently, in tone, they keep to the complexity of the poem's argument. Their logic (as witness my paraphrase above) asserts that unless man becomes truly man – man enough to turn off the time-bomb – the consequence must be that the grizzly bear will take over the world. The irony is, of course, that the men who have set the time-bomb are already "grizzlies," if we credit the speaker's recognition in stanza one.

There would be a certain nemesis if real bears took over a world that had been destroyed by bear-like men. That interpretation, it seems to me, clearly finds its warrant in the first stanza.

The poem is saved from ranting rhetoric, too, because of the ethos of the speaker: he warns not merely the politicians but himself, for the time-bomb is within his own ribs as well. This recognition, this implication of himself, is understated in line 2: he knows the grizzly "in the mirror." He is no aloof prophet of doom.

One cannot ignore the proprieties of form: the prosody and syntax quiet what might have been the frenetic voice of prophecy. Like the angry poem "Status Quo," "Time-Bomb" also uses the ABXB quatrain, but not the full rhymes. The acoustic sparks in the present poem lie quietly under meaning. Moreover, the syntactical parallelisms, from stanza to stanza, seem to offer a form in which the terrible can be seen and understood without the distortions of strong emotions. Each stanza begins with "in" (or "within"), and each of the first two stanzas drives through two predicates. Within this parallelism, a climax is reached in stanza three. Up until now, the subject has been "I"; now the time-bomb itself is subject.

But *Now Is Time* has other voices, some of which are quite different from those of *David*. Quite unique is "Remarks for the Part of Death" (in SP, entitled "Remarks Decoded from Outer Space," p. 145).

In "Young Veterans" (SP, 91), the soldiers now returned home from the war, their memories of the war being erased by the civilian quotidian,

> . . . merge and move with all of us
> toward whatever mystery
> bemused that fatal pliant fish
> who first forgot the sea

The speaker does not say: Men growing into their destinies forget their past selves "just as" the first fish that was to evolve into higher forms of life forgot its marine past. That would be the form of metaphor, or, at least, analogy. The fish here is rather an emblem of a fatedness which moves man as well. Man has his origins in the sea.

That very same theme and symbol fill the whole of "Poem," re-entitled "Flying Fish," in SP, p. 51. As in many poems in this volume, war is figured as the bomber-plane (the "firedrake" of "Time-Bomb"), the dragon of the old myths made anew. The argument of "Flying Fish" may fairly be summarized: Both fish and man attempt flight to escape the terror of a monstrous god of Nemesis; but the air is alien, and they cannot remain in flight; only the devourer can leap comet-like. There are indeed many complementary metaphors, overt and covert – the fish-aviators as dragonflies, as Narcissus, as wards of the sea; the dolphin (a conventional figure for eternity) as fisherman, as scientist, as comet – but the relationship between fish and man remains radically symbolic. Symbolic of what? Of nature's limitations on the wills of its creatures, and symbolic of a god of retribution which pursues those who try to escape their prison.

Doubtless, the most difficult poem in *Now Is Time* is "Lines for a Peace" (SP, 87). It is about the healing of an insane society at the end of the war. Meditating on no concrete scene, the poem rather keeps before our eyes the "cure" of the paranoid. It is a harsh cure; the action is denoted by "flail and bind," "unhook," "crust," "detonate," "shock." This last word capsulates the action in the closing lines:

to bed the beast and with the pain
of love shock him to the brain –
then certify the future sane

Love – not the snake pit or the electric charge – is the painful
shock-treatment that will make society sane. Nor is this closing
paradox fortuitous or merely rhetorical: the poem is fraught
with complementary or paradoxical images of kindness or solici-
tude ("milky") and might, of torture and healing ("flail and
bind"), of uncovering and covering up ("husk") anguish, of the
"leaf's unhuman humours" aiding the human, of the exploding
heart as a "governor" (a device which limits or brakes excessive
speed).

Because there is no concrete scene and no narrative action,
and because this lyric is essentially repetitive in structure, there
is little chance for allegory to root here. Furthermore, despite
the signs of simile (the "as" and the "like"), and despite such
conceits as "the pavement's mind" and "the pavement's yell,"
the poem rests not on metaphor but on symbol. One can readily
see that nature dominates the imagery: sea and waves, fucus (a
kind of seaweed), roots, grasses, leaf, bud, flower.

More important is the implied relationship between nature
and man in his present misery. First of all, nature is not sentimentalized; the waves are milky, but also mighty. The flailing
and binding fucus quiets, "quells," the schizoid water, but as
Birney knows very well, "cwellan" in Old English means "to
kill." Through line 7, fear is a "natural" destroyer-preserver
because it is associated with both the human and inhuman. The
point is made in lines 8 and 9: the "humours" (the bodily
"fluids" which centuries ago were believed to determine a man's
sensibility) are those of the inhuman; it is the life-force of the
leaf, not of the mind, which will give man a direction, a home
for his wandering motives and for his blasted future. The life-
force is nature's. But although much so far in the poem could be
construed as philosphic naturalism, it does not rest in that
theme. Indeed, with l. 12, the poem turns on an abrupt identification (not comparison, but identification): "This heart's a bud
to detonate a flower," and the flower is love. That "heart" and
"flower" – "hearts and flowers" – are conventional metonymies
for "emotion" and "love" is beside the point here. The heart *is*
a bud, for the imagery has, before now, so identified nature and
man that we are urged to accept the bud as a radical symbol.
The closing lines shift to the bedroom, but there is no violation
here. Ironically, the "beast" is not nature, but paranoid man;
and love is both natural and human.

There is, I suppose, much in this poem that one could be

captious about. One could argue that "certify" in the last line admits a clinical and legal tone (the psychiatrist "certifies" a cured patient). It might be that this notion was "meant" to be ironic, yet such an irony seems out of place here. Nevertheless, the poem thoughtfully dramatises its meaning; it is no mere bundle of metaphors.

The angry humanist, attacking complacent attitudes toward war; the ironic, self-aware oracle; the "higher intelligence" from space; the expositor of fate; the physician of the soul, proposing a cure for men made monsters by the war: these are the voices we have heard in *Now Is Time*. The cure for the militant soul is love, and the last major voice is that of the lover.

"This Page My Pigeon" (SP, 88) and "The Road to Nijmegen" (SP, 89) share much the same vision. In them the speakers find in their memory of the beloved the strength which can push back the terror of war. In "The Road to Nijmegen," the woman is remembered as a "tree walking," and the speaker sees through the sleet "the rainbow arch" of her eyes, the covenant of her love. These phantasms rise out of the debris of the devastated city.

Just as fine a poem, and one which more strongly symbolizes the sane naturalness of the beloved, is "This Page My Pigeon." The poem, pushing the metaphor of its title through the first four quatrains, arrives at its destination: the woman at home, and her "meaning." From the beginning it is clear that she represents – symbolizes – the speaker's own life: "My greenest past, my rivered future." The pigeon-poem, likewise, is himself, and the message which the pigeon carried is a creation from out of the midst of war.

> See round his leg snug love's cylinder
> come from this world of wild undoing

The phallic cylinder comes, ironically enough, from a world of de-creation. In this, the early part of the poem, Birney could easily have sentimentalized his imagery. Because the speaker and his beloved are both associated with nature and the things of nature, Birney could have pictured the war as a human crime in which nature plays no part – a "quarrel of iron (man) and growth (nature)." But the "ack-ack" of the anti-aircraft guns are "snake-spit," and the bombers float "like flakes of mica." Indeed, the speaker can even see the bombers both as "beautiful" *and* "brutal." The speaker keeping to this realism, this integrity of feeling, the pigeon flies "Under apathetic suns and over/the pointless ocean." The pun on "pointless" makes it clear that nature has no absolute value in itself, that, rather, it must be pointed by human significance, human reference. (The pointless ocean of nature is, implicitly, opposed by the beloved as the "rivered future" of the speaker.) This implies (remembering that the pigeon's message is a poem – and that the pigeon is a "homer" and Homer) that poetic creation selects from nature; it does not take nature at its own value.

The central metaphor on which the poem ends is one of Birney's happiest choices: the beloved as gardener. She "waters" his memory; her eyes are "leads to the wide light." His loneliness," figured as a "dockweed," "was lopped away long ago burned in your vaulting fire/when first you gardened me." The gardener cares for nature, improves on it, and is not sentimental about destroying weeds. These attitudes authorize the earlier abstractions about the woman as "part of the rightness/of hills[,] the saneness of music and hemlocks." This last phrase suggests that the human ("music") and nature ("hemlocks") are not necessarily opposed. Here, as in "Lines for a Peace," one is made sane by love, and love is both human and natural.

Several poems in *Now Is Time* imply that the earlier distance between man and nature is decreasing in Birney's poetry, and that the earlier opposition between man's order, or man's artifice, and nature's processes is partly resolved. The lover is a poet, and his beloved a gardener. Love serves both man and nature.

5. THE STRAIT OF ANIAN: AFTER THE WAR

It is fortunate that the poem "World War III" had only the one appearance in a volume of Birney's. Its sardonic questionings are answered by its full, ironic rhymes and by its juxtapositions of the ludicrous and the significant. Its deadly whimsy can be seen in the following excerpts:

> Will it be much as before?
> Shall we learn to wear like fraternity pins
> the deaths of our friends once more?
> ....

> Should youth as usual take the hint,
> politely declining to argue with print,
> permitted once more to gouge and smother,
> and still get a weekly blessing from mother?

> Will they save their money and sometimes
>   their lives,
> acquire new skills or noses or wives?
>
>
> Can love bend the earth to his will,
> can we kill only that which drives us to kill,
> and drown our deaths in a Creed?[19]

But by these last, closing lines, any answers that we could have given have withdrawn before the spate of rhetorical questions; the only answer possible is No.

The Strait of Anian, published in 1948, reprints twenty-seven poems from *David* and *Now Is Time*. The nineteen new poems represent the aftermath of the war and Canadian scenes. In this chapter, I want to examine the mood of the several poems which deal with the immediate effects of the war and which speculate on the future. (In the next chapter, I shall survey Birney's "Canadian" poems, his "case history" of Canada.)

Another poem, "Letter to a Possible Great-Grandson," bears a close resemblance to "World War III." Witness the middle three stanzas:

> Some [Young soldiers] acquired shiplore and syphilis,
> learned to keep dapper though drowning;
> a million wandered in tanks tipsily,
> passing out in a swampy morning.
>
> Fat or thin now the survivors
> wear an air as vague as the lost;
> a few are found guilty and filed out for dying,
> but with bandaged eyes look as blank as the rest of us.
>
> The victors goggle at the swelling girth
> of clubs that round the rescued
> (and each other's heads)
> they may not stop from twirling.[20]

Without question, there is some engaging cleverness here: the linking (syllepsis) of "shiplore and "syphilis," the pun on "tanks" (military tanks and local jails), the euphemism for "died" in "passing out."

But one major fault in the poem is its unawareness of the basic situation: the letter to a possible grandson. To make that situation the control on the meaning – and, thus, to create a different meaning – was Birney's task in revising the poem.

"Letter to a Conceivable Great-Grandson" (as the revised poem is entitled in SP, 146) is spoken by one who has lived during the war and during the post-war period of automation. Plainly – and in a more conversational, slangy tone than in the earlier version – the speaker is bedevilled and frustrated by the new machines. It was bad enough, during the war, to have made "our brightest kids into postmen," young men who dropped "aircards" of death; now, automated letters "deliver themselves" (with a notational pun on "de-liver," "deviscerate"). Though the letters and "wholemanuscriptsprepaid" are not explicitly labelled as messages of death, the understatement of the poem makes our feeling that they are death-dealing all the stronger; "push-button warfare" or some label of the kind would have violated the tone and the persona. The speaker (more genuinely in this, the later version of the poem) is even afraid that the present letter will fail to communicate itself to his grandson. What will the grandson use for an "eye"? he asks covertly. And built into his letter are the broken signs of communication: words run together, words broken up into discrete syllables, violations of linear typography.

> But what's crazy for real is
> we're so damned busy no
> body has time to de   what
>   cipher
> language it is we're   iting
>   r
>   w

It might be ventured that the uneasiness about communicating is itself a powerful commentary on men who make war, on the reasons why war is made. If, in the future, men "see" with machines, how will they see with humanity?

"World War III" and the 1948 version of "Letter" are overheated indictments against the past and future of militant men. Birney's talent does not lie, it seems to me, in the discursive poem; it works best within a frame or, better, a symbolic situation. In "Ulysses" (SP, 92) Birney puts Homer's hero into the present, seeing him as a soldier returning home to his wife, a Penelope besieged by suitors with "arms." The poem's address to a contemporary Ulysses is a series of instructions: "Go canny. . . there's no guarantee of an epic ending," the speaker warns. Finally, however, the bow of Ulysses can be strung only by himself, to be used against the 4-F suitors. The tone of the poem plays with the mock-heroic, and yet, all in all, it takes the parallel between the soldier and Ulysses seriously enough.

The four-beat lines and alliterative patterns of this poem are reminiscent of the "Saxon" poems in *David*; in *The Strait of Anian* one finds a fully-fledged Saxon poem, "Mappemounde" (SP, 90). Penelope's suitors are here again, figured as the "mermen/ shore-sneakers who croon to the seafarer's girl/ next year's gleewords." "Mappemounde" describes a map of a flat world and the powers that ruled such a world. Of course, the sea on which sailors return from the war in Europe has been tamed and offers no threat to lives; and yet, as the poem proceeds, it speaks of forces that can seduce the girls back home, that can dry up her tears and burn up the memory of her sailor-lover, that can destroy the sailor's pledges of love. "That sea is hight [named] time," time which effaces the heart's promises made on land. Terrified and adrift on that sea, we reach "map's end" and, thus, the death of our love. The emblems of the winds and the monsters on the old maps are symbols here of the fatefulness of time and of loss. Compared to Birney's other "Saxon" poems, "Mappemounde," in its persuasive use of its symbols, easily rivals "War Winters" and, in my opinion, surpasses "Anglosaxon Street."

"Man Is a Snow" and its companion poem, ". . . Or a Wind" are among Birney's most powerful and successful poems. Instead of using the more immediately ironic and contemporaneous attacks on militant men – as in "World War III" and in the 1948 version of "Letter" – Birney has abstracted the postwar situation into potent symbols. The two poems give different answers to man's hope for the future, and each answer is controlled and deeply argued. (It would be instructive to do a complete comparison between the early and the 1966 versions of "Man Is a Snow," but we will keep pretty much to the text of the SP version.)

The 1948 version of "Man Is a Snow" begins with the lines:

> I tell you the wilderness we fell
> is nothing to the one we breed.[21]

That contrast governs the whole poem. The destruction and domestication of the wilderness is as nothing compared to "the rotograved lie/and a nursery of crosses abroad."

> Not the cougar leaping to myth
> from the orange lynx of our flame
> not the timber swooning to death

in the shock of the saw's bright whine
but the rotograved lie
and a nursery of crosses abroad [SP, 148]

The death of wild animals has at least passed into myth and, thus, remains meaningful; and the fire with which the pioneers cleared the land for cultivation is itself a wild thing, a "lynx." The saw's whine is (synesthetically) "bright." In the last two lines here, effects which might have been merely momentary and rhetorical are wholly involved in the stanza. The notational pun in "rotograved" suggests something like "mechanically repeated and superficially beautiful" – a Norman Rockwell cover-picture of a military cemetery; and, likewise, the pun on "nursery" of crosses also suggests the domestication, the euphemistic evasion, of death. These meanings precisely contrast, on common ground, with the death of cougars and trees. The second stanza continues in much the same way: the man-sown wheat replacing the prairie-grass is not so terrible a change as the harvest left to rot because of man's doubt and his hoarding. ("The starved in the hour of our hoarding" – perhaps a twist on "at the hour of our death", in the Ave Maria – is a very fine paradox.)

It is clear by now that man's denaturalization of nature, his pollution of its waters, is radically symbolic of his dehumanization of himself:

not the rivers we foul but our blood
o cold and more devious rushing

This kind of nature symbolism recalls that of the earlier poems "Flying Fish" and "Lines for a Peace": Birney has written his best poems, it seems to me, within this intuition. In many other poems, the targets – romantically aimed at, for all the strength of the rhetoric – are human institutions and the cultus of Mars. But there is no such sentimentality in "Man Is a Snow," for here man has entombed himself. The poem shrinks man's society down to himself, and then continues its nature symbolism:

Man is a snow that cracks
the trees' red resinous arches
and winters the cabined heart
till the chilled nail shrinks in the wall
and pistols the brittle air
till frost like ferns of the world that is lost
unfurls on the darkening window

Symbols, of course, do not alone a poem make: the syntax and prosody of "Man Is a Snow" do their work. Notice that the first grammatical predication does not come until 1. 13: "Man is a snow. . . ." Every image that precedes 1. 13 is preparation for this, the climatic, identification. But neither are those images all a jumble: they are controlled by a quite rigid, schematic syntax. The basic scheme, abstracted, looks something like this:

   (1) Not the cougar leaping
   (3) not the timber swooning
   (5) but the rotograved lie
   (6) and a nursery
   (7) Not the death
   (9) but the harvest
  (10) and the starved
  (11) not the rivers . . . but our blood.

Lines 2, 4, and 8 modify lines 1, 3, and 7. The syntax in the closing stanza is almost as schematic. Counterpointing the rigid syntax is the flowing anapestic rhythm of the trimeter lines, heard clearly in the following:

       x   x   / | x   x / | x   x   /
   (6) and a nursery of crosses abroad

       x   x   / |x x   / | x x   / |x
  (10) and the starved in the hour of our hoarding

      /   x   / | x x   / | x   x   /
  (11) not the rivers we foul but our blood

iambs and, in a few cases, spondees (//) are substituted for anapests, but it is the anapestic cadence we hear most strongly. The tension between the rhythm and the syntax may be taken, I submit, as a formal equivalence of the tensions created by the images. Craft is one with meaning.

Apparently written about a year after its companion poem, ". . . Or a Wind" (SP, 149) dissipates the despair and ecstatically hopes in a new freedom for man. Soldiers returning home are like "a puff of wind from the sea. . . met by the cliffs of a continent," and that comparison is maintained throughout the poem. The winds "coil upon" themselves, snakelike, and threaten to "dissipate" (a play on the moral meaning of "dissipation"); and yet suffering ("acid tears") may win out over the mountain walls. The "hail of our wills" may batter the rock and give us our freedom. The last verse-paragraph is full of verbal energy:

O we may yet roar free   unwhirl
sweeping great waves into the deepening bores
bringing the ocean to boom and fountain and
    siren
tumbling the fearful clouds into a great sky
    wallowing
cracking the mountain apart
the great wind of humanity blowing free blowing
    through
streaming over the future

It is impossible to assign precise allegorical meanings to this
poem, and that is, perhaps, a measure of its success. Birney has
abstracted the feelings at the end of the war into a symbolic
parable that transcends the rational definitions of allegory. The
poem does not tell us what to think about those feelings so
much as it represents the doubts and the willful optimism about
man's future after the war.

Returning to "Mappemounde," one can understand that Birney, as a student of Old English poetry, could not have failed to
try his hand at imitating the Anglo-Saxon verse-line. But apart
from the student-poet, there is perhaps a connexion between
Birney's attitudes toward nature and those of the scop. In
Northrop Frye's essay "La Tradition Narrative dans la Poésie
Canadienne-Anglaise," he suggests that in certain Old English
poems – in "The Wanderer" and "The Seafarer" – there is a
way of feeling which to a modern reader seems more Canadian
than English – a feeling of melancholy in a sparsely colonized
country, a feeling of terrible solitude in the poet of that country,
a feeling of resignation to misery and to lonesomeness as the
only way of achieving, if not serenity, at least a sort of austere
calm.[22] Although Birney's "Saxon" poems present the mock-
heroic, they assume the existence of the heroic and of myth,
myth on the scale of the scop's kennings; and these poems suggest something of the loneliness or terror of the poet in a country which owes little to the "ministration of man." That is the
prevailing feeling in many of Birney's "Canadian" poems, to
which I now turn.

6. CANADA: CASE HISTORY

The title-poem of "Canada: Case History" (the fourth section of *Selected Poems*) is a misleading guide to the journeys of the poet; neither its mock-clinical tone, nor its synecdoche of the Canadian teenager, nor its political and cultural satire are typical of the form and matter of Birney's travels in Canada. Moreover, that this group of poems is a "chronicle" of Canada is also a distraction.[23] The Canadian people, their cultures and their politics, are almost wholly contained within the nature of their land; and the symbols rising out of the landscape, or sometimes imposed on the landscape by the traveller, suggest a comprehension of Canada quite unlike that of the traditional chronicler. Metonomy, the land for the people of the land, is Birney's master trope.

But the notion that Birney has chronicled Canada is defective for two more relevant and related motives. First, the ethos of the speakers is dominant in many of these poems: the land doesn't easily give up its secrets, but must be interpreted by metaphor. Although the poems are sometimes impersonal enough, often the speaker strains to wrestle meanings from the land. This urgency, as in "North Star West" and "Way to the West," calls as much attention to the traveller as it does to the substance of his accounts. Second, the traveller is frustrated by the lack of what I might here call public metonomies. Canada is a mythless, storyless country. At the beginning of "North of Superior" (*SP*, 112), Birney writes:

> Not here the ballad or the human story
> the Scylding boaster or the water-troll
> not here and mind   only the soundless fugues
> of stone   the leaf and lake   where but the brutish
> ranges   big with haze   confine the keyboard

Contrasted with the heroic and romantic myths of older countries, Canadian poetry must make original responses to its land, and for the man who loves and teaches Old- and Middle-English poetry, the lack of myths in his own country is a terrible challenge. Birney cannot accept the universal myths of a T. S. Eliot or the copybook national myths of a Hart Crane; nor can he accept the world seen by William Carlos Williams and Wallace Stevens, a world without large, racial, public myths.

My point here is simply that in the "Canadian" poems there is a real tension between the will to discover or impose myth and the realization that "the breeze/today shakes blades of light without a meaning" (*SP*, 112); the rains and dews of Canada have no chthonic father. Pulled by these motives, no poet can, I think, write chronicles. North of Lake Superior, the poet is "guilty" in his having brought his humanity into an inhuman land.

Man is often smaller than human size, and his "great ships are scattered twigs/on [the] green commotion" of the sea, his plane "a fugitive mote/in the stare of the sun" (*SP*, 96). The sea, as well as the land, passes through its cycles of birth and death "without ministration of man." Within the *anima* and *animus* of nature, people live out their desires, ignorant of "the simple unhuman truth of this emptiness." "Atlantic Door" and "Gulf of Georgia" bare the need to "wash your mind of its landness," to discover the nonhuman "other" of nature, the destructive element.

The danger, of course, lies in the human's becoming wholly absorbed by the processes of nature. In "The Ebb Begins from Dream" (*SP*, 108), Toronto workers "ebb" back to their jobs in the morning, and in the evening "flood" homeward. Granted the ingenuity that enforces (or forces) the metaphor throughout the poem, the "relentless moon" symbolizes the power that controls the ebb and flow of nature and of man. In the womb of nature, man "dreams of vaster wellings" than the neaptide of nature will allow. Man limited by his environment is also the theme of "Winter Saturday" (*SP*, 114). In a note on this poem, Birney wrote that it is held together by "a single image which likens the family to a caterpillar changing into a cocoon and, under the stimulus of the town's light and heat, into a moth."[24]

The most terrifying of these poems is "Bushed" (SP, 117) – one of Birney's best poems, I believe.

> He invented a rainbow but lightning struck it
> shattered it into the lake-lap of a mountain
> so big his mind slowed when he looked at it
>
> Yet he built a shack on the shore
> learned to roast porcupine belly and
> wore the quills on his hatband

At first he was out with the dawn
whether it yellowed bright as wood-columbine
or was only a fuzzed moth in a flannel of storm
But he found the mountain was clearly alive
sent messages whizzing down every hot morning
boomed proclamations at noon and spread out
a white guard of goat
before falling asleep on its feet at sundown

When he tried his eyes on the lake   ospreys
would fall like valkyries
choosing the cut-throat
He took then to waiting
till the night smoke rose from the boil of the sunset

But the moon carved unknown totems
out of the lakeshore
owls in the beardusky woods derided him
moosehorned cedars circled his swamps and tossed
their antlers up to the stars
Then he knew   though the mountain slept   the winds
were shaping its peak to an arrowhead
poised

And now he could only
bar himself in and wait
for the great flint to come singing into his heart.

In *The Creative Writer* (pp. 29-30), Birney has written a very interesting account of the transformations of this poem over several drafts, of his discovery of the true poem. His motive was originally to write a satire on two greenhorn professors who fatuously thought that one could live in an isolated mountain cabin, during atomic war, if the cabin were equipped with a radio and canned food. After an attempt to let the professors themselves betray their ignorance about solitude, Birney remembered seeing, as a boy, the corpse of an old trapper who starved himself to death. "Bushed," Birney's father commented at the time. "The woods got him, the loneliness." Remembering that moment, Birney, thirty-five years later, discovered his poem.

Or almost. For one thing, Birney must have had to consider the role of the speaker of the poem. A wholly disengaged voice (like that of "The Ebb Begins from Dream" and "Winter Saturday") might have thrown too many ironies against the trapper's situation; on the other hand, a wholly inside view would not have allowed the speaker insight into the crazed mind of the trapper. The solution, it seems to me, is a voice which mediates (or perhaps transcends) both possibilities. The focus is on the trapper's actions, illusions, and recognitions; and yet the speaker is always in control (the logical signals of "yet," "but," "then," "now" indicate as much).

The quietly controlled point of view in the poem is no mean achievement, but an even finer skill, perhaps, is in the imagery itself. Except for a few instances, the images are of the trapper's mountain world; where the images are external to that world – as in the "messages" and "proclamations" sent out by the mountain, or in the ospreys "like valkyries" – one is persuaded (just how I don't know) that they articulate the trapper's own awareness.

The amazing thing is the resonance achieved by the poem's imagery. An omen of destruction comes at the very beginning of the poem:

> He invented a rainbow but lightning struck it
> shattered it into the lake-lap of a mountain
> so big his mind slowed when he looked at it

Whether or not the rainbow is the conventional (and Biblical) emblem of God's covenant with man, or just a popular image of beauty, the key word here is "invented": the lightning shatters a creation wrought by man. The lightning and the rainbow are so much, and immediately, part of the psychic world of the isolated trapper that one doesn't call them into question as "metaphors." Just as impressive are the consequences of his having invented a rainbow: lightning strikes the rainbow, which shatters into the lake-lap of a mountain, a mountain so big that the trapper's mind had to slow down when he looked at it. Mysteriously, the last line itself suggests the power of the mountain over the trapper: the object determines the very act of seeing it; and it tacitly comments on the feeble power of the trapper's "invention" of an unreal rainbow. The lightning as the symbol of nature's strength destroys man's attempt to re-create what belongs properly to nature.

But the trapper lives: he builds a shelter, learns how "to roast porcupine belly," and ornaments his hatband with the porky's quills. In this, the second, verse-paragraph, we are suddenly and casually given an account of the trapper's routine – and that is the point. After the shattering of the rainbow-illusion, the trapper nevertheless manages to live, even to achieve a small mastery over nature. (That "small" is not the speaker's own word – that he withholds comment on what is suggested here – indicates once again his awareness of his role in the poem.)

But the trapper cannot master the mountain; it is not only "alive" but articulate. It sends "messages," booms out "proclamations," and sets its goats as guards. The metaphor, in line 2, of the "lake-lap of a mountain" may have seemed arbitrary, whimsical, but it actually anticipates the split-personification of the mountain in paragraph three. By "split-personification" (a term sometimes used to describe a peculiar figure in romantic poetry), I mean that the mountain is both a "real" mountain and one which to the impressionable, lonely trapper also possesses human abilities. (And animal traits as well: it falls asleep "on its feet.")

Eventually the trapper cannot bear to be outside his cabin during daylight. The mountain speaks, but its "messages" proclaim words which the trapper either cannot understand or doesn't wish to understand. Nor is the lake a place of refuge for his eyes or a source of food during the daylight hours. The fish are, or course, "cut-throat trout," but, granted the pun, they are also the slain whom the valkyries choose and conduct to Valhalla. The ospreys as the valkyries do the killing, and the trapper must wait until nightfall, "till the night smoke rose from the boil of the sunset." This line looks back, I think, to the trapper's cooking in paragraph two: now, nature boils, and animals kill animals. Deepening, his obsessions turn to totemism:

> But the moon carved unknown totems
> out of the lakeshore
> owls in the beardusky woods derided him
> moosehorned cedars circled his swamps and tossed
> their antlers up to the stars.

Representing the Indian's animistic beliefs and the power of his clan, the carved totem becomes the very emblem of primitive death: the arrowhead, the mountain peak which here the wind shapes. The trapper awaits the "great flint to come singing into his heart." (That flint is used to make fire suggests a connotative bond with the earlier images of the lightning and sun.)

Another carefully crafted and charming poem is "From the Hazel Bough." Written in dimeter lines and in quatrain stanzas, it neatly escapes jingle usually by alternating rising meters (in the even-numbered lines) with falling, spondaic [//], or amphimacer [hazel eyes] substitutions. A tender poem, it pursues its nature imagery in a wonderfully naif tone right to the understated ending:

> but no man sees
>   where the trout lie now
> or what leans out
>   from the hazel bough [SP, 107]

"Aluroid" (SP, 131), which Birney interprets in *The Creative Writer* (pp. 20-23), shows another success in his handling of the short line. And the whole irony of that poem rests in the sudden way in which the almost archetypal cat becomes the domesticated pussy once again. For once, nature doesn't be-wild man.

The drive toward human order (which is what myth is all about) is very strong in the Canadian poems. Within it, Birney attacks the violations of nature by human disorder, by man's machines and factories (as in "Way to the West" and "Images in Place of Logging")' The poem "Page of Gaspé," extending the conceit of its title, figures the transformation of the rural landscape in its closing lines:

> But a later hand has added above the oxcart
> two squat banks and an oblong factory
>
> Daily now over the Gaspé landpage
> grown up children scribble
> the smoke of transient trains
> and chalk the aimless graffiti of jetplanes

The "scribble" of modern man contrasts with the earlier "human typelines"; however, whether the irony works for or against the poem, it is a little difficult to see why lines of type should be more "human" than a "scribble." But the emphasis in such words as "transient," "aimless," "smoke," and "chalk" is clear enough: the Gaspé landpage is being written over by a disordered, rootless, ephemeral, mechanized society.

"North Star West" is a clever poem with many arresting lines:

> we fix the individual light   the common thought
>
> our destinies fixed but our seats adjusta*ble*
> airvents person*al*   discretion gener*al*
> we *lie* like *l*ambs in the *l*ion of sc*ie*nce. [Italics mine]

A wonderfully underplayed mock-heroic couplet:

> The professor overbids and goes down three
> His mother orders buttered scones and tea.

And when (as at the beginning of the poem) the speaker interjects allusions to myths, there is usually the tone of highjinksing hyperbole. The never-ending hunt for metaphor becomes tedious from time to time, but the poem earns the right to its closing lines – perhaps among the best in Birney's poetry.

> Yet for a space we held in our morning's hand
> the welling and wildness of Canada   the fling of a nation
> We who have ridden the wings of our people's cunning
> and lived in a star at peace among stars
> return to our ferment of earth with a memory of sky

As this poem suggests, the search for human order is severely tested in the Canadian poems; in them, the destination is perhaps never reached. Nonetheless, the search is real and urgent, and Birney was to do more travelling.

7. WORLD TRAVELS

In 1955, after finishing *Down the Long Table* (his second novel), Birney travelled in Mexico, returning home the next year. During the 1958-59 academic year, he journeyed westward: Hawaii, Japan, Hong Kong, Thailand, India, London – often giving poetry readings at colleges. The poems rising from those travels were published in *Ice Cod Bell or Stone*, in 1962. On sabbatical leave and appointed Senior Arts Fellow by the Canada Council for 1962-63, Birney started out again: Mexico, the West Indies, Venezuela, Colombia, Peru, Chile, Argentina, Greece, Spain, London. *Near False Creek Mouth* (1964) contained his new poems.

Reading Canadian poetry was the official job of this, in John Robert Colombo's phase, poetic ambassador. But in the poems, the tourist overwhelms the official and assumes many roles: the amused listener for native hucksters; the reflective and, at times, self-conscious foreigner; the joyous discoverer of large myths, writ small or big in what he sees, the lonely, irritated, appealing, ironic, patronizing, thankful, frightened, humble man. Despite the many personae in these poems, one comes to feel, reading them, that Birney has finally recorded his own voice, his own sensibility. In retrospect, the earlier poems seem to force metaphor and myth into service at the expense of personality. Could one say of the "Saxon" poems, or of "Dusk on the Bay," or "Takkakaw Falls" that they sound totally like Birney's own voice, and his alone? A.J.M. Smith puts the matter more strongly: Birney's earlier poems "for all their sincerity and accuracy . . . speak with the voices of Auden, Rex Warner, or Stephen Spender."[25] Not that we ever learn anything about the speaker's "character" – he never *does* anything fateful; but we do hear the inflections of his voice and see a great deal through his moral and mythical eye.

The poem "Can. Lit." (in ICBoS, not in SP) ends with the line,

> It's only by our lack of ghosts we're haunted.

Canada has no viable myths, and no Emily Dickinsons and Walt Whitmans. Yet, it is a mistake to believe that Birney turned into a student of the myths of other countries; certainly he is no amateur anthropologist in his travel poems. Though he is aware of the history of the country he visits, his emphasis is on a present realization. Rarely bookish, he always attempts to let a present experience shape itself into meaning. The structure of many of the travel poems is anecdotal, but anecdote not altogether bound by the local circumstances.

"The Bear on the Delhi Road" (SP, 14) pictures the attempt of two Kashmiris to train a huge Himalayan bear to dance for their living. The men, "spindly as locusts," are peaceful without joy in the hot dust, jumping out of reach of the bear's claws. But the poem does not turn to a tone of grotesque comedy or of pity for the dancers; the description, despite the few metaphors, is cool matter of fact.

> They have not led him here
> down from the fabulous hills
> to this bald alien plain
> and the clamorous world   to kill
> but simply to teach him to dance

The bear does, however, grow in meaning throughout the poem. At the beginning he is "Unreal tall as a myth," but that is the insight of the tourist who has not yet brooded on the relations within the scene. The bear itself seems to become less than the unreal creature from the "fabulous hills"; the Kashmiris dance

          . . . merely to wear   wear
    from his shaggy body the tranced
    wish forever to stay
    only an ambling bear
    four-footed in berries

– "only" sees the bear as bear: the speaker doesn't fool himself
about the bear as an unreal myth, but respects the trainers'
view.

   And yet he transcends that view. "It is not easy to free myth
from reality": he suggests that the bear as myth and the bear as
commercial property cannot be detached from the other. The
"tranced" bear and "the tranced dancing of men" share an act
which is one and whole, both mythic and actual, both nonhuman and human. The earlier polyptoton admits as much: "the
bear alive is their living."

   In many of the travel poems, there is an amused distrust of
hoked-up myths and of the commercial bait for tourists: the
garbled vulgarity of the native booster of "Hononulu" (SP, 6),
the old ram feigning neglect at the dispassionate hands of the
shepherdess of "Twenty-Third Flight" (SP, 3), the modern con-
veniences offered to the theatre-goer at "Epidaurus" (SP, 16),
the native speaker's preference for bulldozers over romantic
machetes and local beauty in "Sinaloa" (SP, 40). Although Birney isn't sucked into the world of the local Tourist Office, his is
rarely the tone of the outraged highbrow: there's a good earthy
acceptance of the *guía tourista*. Often funny and sometimes hi-
larious, some of these poems make a discovery beyond finding
oneself amused. In the theatre at Epidaurus, after the announce-
ment that the tourist's comforts will be served,

    Everybody however
    still waits to
    hear the
    pin
    dr
    o
    p

– there is still the ageless, breathless pause before the play begins.†

† Mr. Birney writes: "The immediate reference is to the habit of guides at
Epidaurus making their tourists climb up to the top benches and sit in
silence while the guide stands in the centre of the 'orchestra' and drops a
pin. It can be heard . . . ."

The travel poems – all of them, I believe – respect one imperative: a myth, even for the tourist, must live in one's experience. A human myth cannot be detached from the reality of which it is part. In "Tavern by the Hellespont" (SP, 15), the allusive ghosts of Alexander, Xenophon, Hero and Leander, and Byron offer no company for the lone and lonely speaker. The radio's Hollywood cowboy song in "Transistor" puts a distance between the young couple on the porch and the old woman who sings the old songs of Jamaica.

Perhaps the act which most expresses the real-as-myth (as I might call it) in the travel poems is ritual movement: the dance. In "Sestina for Tehuantepec" (SP, 48), the swaying ritual walk of the matriarchs, carrying their fruit and iguanas, comprises an order beyond politics, and deeper than nature itself. In "For George Lamming" (SP, 52), Birney, at a party given by the author of *In the Castle of My Skin*, is caught up in the dance of "black tulip faces/self swaying forgotten" only to see himself suddenly in a mirror," like a white snail/in the supple dark flowers." The closing tribute to the Jamaicans is expressed in the terms of movement:

> Always now I move grateful
>   to all of you
> who let me walk thoughtless
>   and unchallenged
> in the gardens
>   in the castles
>   of your skins

That poem and, more especially, "Bangkok Boy" (SP, 12) suggest that the intersection of myth and reality, of forever and the "dazzled instant," is not in stylized but in spontaneous dance. The little Thai "makes a jig up" that is associated with the life force of the sun. His rhythms deny, the speaker thinks, the stillness of stone Buddhas, the "splayed [awkward because stylized] gyrations of temple dancers," and the "grave measures" of tourists. Repeated references to jazz terms (the terms here are a little dated, perhaps) suggest the improvisations of jazz rhythms in the boy's dance.

> Scamper little Thai
> hot on these hot stones
> scat   leap
> this is forever

I'd venture that "scat" doesn't mean "go away" so much as "dance as the scat singer sings." Both dancer and singer use gesture, rather than "words," so that they may improvise freely, or, in the case of the singer, imitate an instrument that can exceed the possibilities of the human voice. In the boy's dance, "the bright/sun [is] caught/cool."

The first two sections in *Selected Poems* mostly reprint the poems of *Ice Cod Bell or Stone* (1962) and *Near False Creek Mouth* (1964); but these sections also reprint several poems which were written before 1953. Among them are "Introvert," "Transcontinental," "Leaving the Park," "Oldster," "Flying Fish," and "St. Valentine Is Past." The structures, tones, and subjects of these older poems make them stand apart from their younger companions.

What distinguishes these older poems is that each commits itself, almost from the very beginning, to the elaboration of a radical metaphor and/or a single tone. The poems hammer away at their conceits, drawing them out until they almost break. Playing off nature and man, the language plays with words; the puns point to the nature and to man.

> His mind to him is tight as any park
> where thoughts like raddled ducks are pulled
> by lines unsensed   on water ruled.
>
> ["Introvert," SP, 20]

> Crawling across this sometime garden
> now in our chaircars like clever nits
> in a plush caterpillar . . .
>
> ["Transcontinental," SP, 25]

> we may rifle flowers now
>   blow flowers from rifles
>
> ["Leaving the Park," SP, 30]

> He has grown old as poplars do
> dappling somehow – the green sheen spent –
> his olive hide with a pithy comment of scars
>
> ["Oldster," SP, 31]

As I have argued earlier in this essay, "Flying Fish" is something more than an extended conceit, but that figure is basis for the whole poem. "St. Valentine Is Past" – quite unique among Birney's poems – is a myth in which the four primal elements (earth, air, water, and fire) play ascending and descending roles.

Whatever the virtues of these poems, Birney keeps a tight rein on their metaphors, and on their commanding, witty tone. The speakers and third-person subjects represent not persons individualized in time and space but, rather, symbols of oldsters, lovers, introverts, a land like a diseased old woman.

On the other hand, and more often than not, the newer travel poems hold their images and metaphors in suspension until the last. Instead of elaborating conceits, they move dramatically through concrete descriptions and tentative metaphors to a final revelation. That epiphany – whether it be the sight of a small boy flying a kite, or a ten-foot pair of concrete shoes, or a spear piercing Captain Cook – suddenly gives significance to the randomness of the earlier observations. The tourist's experience becomes something more than an anecdote.

"A Walk in Kyoto" (p. 10) begins with the tourist at his inn. He is told by the maid that the time is "Boy's Day," "Man's Day." The occidental really doesn't know what is being celebrated. Is the magnolia sprig in his alcove a symbol of the male principal? "The ancient discretions of Zen were not shaped/for my phallic western eye"; and the maid's own discretions leave him "clueless." A synecdoche for Japan, the maid's "wild hair of waterfalls [has been] combed straight/in the ricefields": traditions have domesticated the wildness of nature.

In "Cartagena de Indias" (p. 59) the speaker is an invader, "tall as a demon" in the eyes of the poor, and approached by them only because he may buy their wares and services. Wandering among the brotherhood of the poor and diseased, he thinks:

> Somewhere there must be a bridge
> from my stupid wish
> to their human acceptance
> but what can I offer –
> my tongue half-locked in the cell
> of its language – other than pesos
> . . . .
> as I clump unmaimed
> in the bright shoes
> that keep me from hookworm
> lockjaw and snakebite

The "bridge," of course, turns out to be the memorial to the town's poet, Luis Lopez: a pair of old shoes, concrete and ten feet long. The speaker, as it were, casts off his much-polished shoes and accepts the shoes of deadman Luis. The town comes alive with meaning in the love which it has for its critical but loving poet.

"Cartagena de Indias" rests not on metaphor but on life seen and felt by a foreigner. Unlike "A Walk in Kyoto" there are few transformations of images and metaphors. Nor is there that resonance of images that one can find in "Captain Cook" (p. 4), a poem which patiently repeats images – the shilling (and the six tuppennies), the javelin, the Strait of Anian leading to England, the mouths, the birds – until the full irony of Cook's life is completed in his death. No matter where he may voyage, the explorer is accompanied by death, masked or unmasked, slow or sudden.

Birney imposes no anecdotal grid over his experiences. At times, a few allusions point the meaning which is otherwise there in the action; in "Pachucan Miners," the Orphic miners descend the silver mountain to their nightly rescue of Eurydice. In some poems, including the very fine "Machu Picchu," the speaker is projected into myth only through meditating on past and present. There are, too, some lucky moments, as in "Barranquilla Bridge," when the actors in the scene compose a meaning which resists metaphor and which is a universal in itself. Whatever the form of the travel poems, they are rarely "sermons-from-stones poems." This is Hayden Carruth's epithet, and witnesses his notion that Birney, at the end of a poem, "tacks on his own feeling about what he has described, usually sociological in nature." And getting to the "application" section of Birney's sermon is, Mr. Carruth feels, often a laborious process: "Many of his poems have the air of having been 'worked up' from meagre beginnings. . . ."[26]

This simply isn't true, or even valid. There is nothing sententious about Birney's poems, and in fact the "working up" is the act of meditation itself. Birney-as-speaker usually acknowledges his limitations – as in "Machu Picchu" and the "Kyoto" poem – and works to transcend them. And when he generalizes – as in the last verse paragraph of "Barranquilla Bridge" – he doesn't try to nucleate the theme of the poem so much as offer an analogy which puts the scene into ironic perspective.

> It's the sort of rough justice
> the weak can perform on powers above
> (Passers of counterfeit would agree
> – and in Barranquilla   hunger
> fortifies Gresham's Law)

"Sort of," the play on "rough" and "powers above," and the excessive weight of "Gresham's Law" suggest a playful tone which, of course, few preachers would entertain. Moreover, even if one, stretching the point, agrees that these lines "tack on" Birney's own feelings, hasn't that feeling been felt earlier in the poem? In describing the boys' catching the floating fruit in their wire baskets, the speaker says:

> But you can't tell good from bad
> when they're swirling in muddy waters
> whoever you are
> till you've rescued them all

The tone here is not unlike that of the closing paragraph. "Good" and "bad" abstract from the scene much as "justice" does later on, and "rescued" whispers hyperbole in the manner of the last paragraph. The "you" in the lines above is the colloquial version of the impersonal pronoun "one"; and yet it indicates that the speaker, suddenly changing the point of view from the third person, is identifying with the boys as well as universalizing them.

No, Mr. Carruth's account doesn't stand up against an audit. Granting that one poem is not the only piece of evidence, it seems to me that when a travel poem fails it fails because it is not "worked up" *enough*, or it fails because Birney sees only through the eye of irony. "Hot Springs" (p. 45) is about cold rich old buzzards paying for heat from young chicks. The spa which once served Montezuma now serves old lechers. The poor old goatherders, on the other side of the street, are also lecherous, but it costs them nothing "with their fiery old eyes... casually [to] strip the arriving ladies." The tone alternates "wheeeee," the gutsy "or to put it straight on the line," and the heavy ironic Latinity of the ladies coming "only to render/ supplementary thermal assistance." A little funny for the first reading, "Hot Springs" doesn't tell us any more about Mexico than the legend on honeymoon cars: "New York this morning, Hot Springs tonight." At times Birney is not above playing the smart aleck. The targets, moveover, are usually sitting ducks: the ignorant, reactionary commoner of "Billboards Build Freedom of Choice," the poseur poetaster in "London Poetry Pub," the evangelist in "Mammorial Stanzas for Aimée Simple McFarcin," the eternal North-American drunken bum artist in "Ajijic."

But perhaps these are only exercises for the free spirit that has made "Letter to a Cuzco Priest" (p. 66) and the fine "El Greco:

Espolio" (p. 18). As in "Machu Picchu," "Letter" uses anti-phonal structure, indicated by the groups of lines at the margin and by those that are indented. Birney's addresses to the rebel priest alternate with descriptions of a brutal incident and its aftermath. The pathos of the Indians' futile, necessary opposi-tion to Establishment guns is matched by the paradoxical tone of the addresses to the priest. The language of address is reli-gious, but the matter insists that the divine flame is in man and not in god, who is perfect. Priest and Indian peasant, both victims, are identified:

> Father   gullible and noble
> born to be martyred
> and to be the worthy instrument
> of the martyrdom of the gullible

As I suggested in commenting on "Bushed," the success of that poem lies in the speaker's point of view, which is both, and at the same time, external and internal. That is just as true of the poem on El Greco's magnificent *Espolio*. Clearly, what drew Birney's eyes was the carpenter, "working alone in that firm and profound abstraction," in that prudence of art and craft and muscular strength which is his only faith. He is the center of the painting and of the poem.

But the painting isn't the poem: El Greco hasn't done Bir-ney's work for him. To get right down to it: the poet could have seen the carpenter as artist from any one of several viewpoints. The carpenter himself could have been the speaker, but a mono-logue would probably have cast him too much as an individual; besides, in the poem, the carpenter is not quite conscious of things and people which could distract him from his work – people and things which in the painting and in the poem "frame" the carpenter. On the other hand, some kind of wholly third-person viewpoint might have risked weighting the carpen-ter's work with too much "symbolism,"or, at least, weighing the worker's own motives too lightly. What is needed, and what the poem does actually achieve, is a point of view which will present the work as the carpenter understands it, and which nevertheless is not wholly restricted to that understanding. Speaking about Birney's monologues and mimicry (about such a poem as "Sin-alóa"), Paul West says something which applies as well to "El Greco: *Espolio*": "The mimicry is the lunge out of oneself, the effort to transpose oneself without however losing the advan-tages of intelligence."[27]

The carpenter is intent on the pressure of his hand
on the awl   and the trick of pinpointing his strength
through the awl to the wood   which is tough
He has no effort to spare for despoilings
or to worry if he'll be cut in on the dice
His skill is vital to the scene   and the safety of the state
Anyone can perform the indignities   It's his hard arms
and craft that hold the eyes of the convict's women
There is the problem of getting the holes exact
(in the middle of this elbowing crowd)
and deep enough to hold the spikes
after they've sunk through those bared feet
and inadequate wrists he knows are waiting behind him

Line 9 begins impersonally with a prop subject and "problem,"
and the remaining lines describe the nature of the problem. But
from whose view? In what way does the carpenter "know"? It
would seem that these lines attempt to describe not the conscious "thinking" of the carpenter but rather the purpose of his
work which "he knows" intuitively. He may well have already
noticed the "inadequate wrists" of Christ; and, knowing that
they are those of a carpenter's son, he may have been struck by
the irony of his own "hard arms. Yet, this isn't quite relevant;
the impersonal tone keeps the focus on the practice of the carpenter. There is perhaps only one intrusion on the part of the
speaker: "It's his hard arms/and craft that hold the eyes of the
convict's women." Even here, however, one doesn't have the
impression that the speaker is looking at a picture; the concre-
tion of "hold" and the situation's own label of "convict" for
Christ suggests that the speaker is himself projected into the
scene. The language – marvellously adjusted to the point of view
– manages to smuggle in (ever so quietly) the ironies of the
situation. The diction balances the formal and the colloquial in
"despoilings," "indignities," "vital to the scene and the safety of
the state," and, on the other hand, "the trick of," and "cut in
on the dice." And if the ear hears "all" for "awl" in line 2, I'm
sure Birney would not object. Only "trick" jars a little – it may
be the one mistake in the whole poem. The colloquialism suits
the tone, but is the connotation of the carpenter as trickster to
be entertained?
  The speculation in the next three lines seems once again to be
another intrusion – an image of the poet looking at El Greco's
picture. But in the fourth line the speaker restores the focus on
the carpenter's habits of thought.

He doesn't sense perhaps that one of the hands
is held in a curious gesture over him –
giving   or asking   forgiveness? –
but he'd scarcely take time to be puzzled by poses

The word "curious," the abstraction of the word "gesture," and the questioning tone offer a perspective which doesn't come from one who has lived in the Christian tradition. (The four lines represent almost total change over the version in *Ice Cod Bell or Stone*. The new word "gesture" for the earlier "beseech-ment" seems to bear out my interest in point of view: "beseech-ment," much more interpretive than "gesture," is thus a more intrusive word.)

The rest of the poem attempts, in part, to mime *what might have been* the reaction of the carpenter to Christ and to the rightness of his craft.

Well heres a carpenter's son who'll have carpenter sons
God willing   and build what's wanted   temples
    or tables
mangers or crosses   and shape them decently
working alone in that firm and profound abstraction

The last five words here are not, of course, the carpenter's own, but by now the tone can accommodate such an intrusion.

Since most of us live in Christianity – whether we profess belief in it or not – the rhetorical problem remains: what ironies, if any, may the carpenter be held in account for? Is the artist's abstraction sometimes too profound? These questions are, I think, too weighty for one poem. It pictures not the Magus of Eliot's poem but a decent, honest, common man, who would live and beget sons in a society which is perhaps rotten but which must go on.

Whatever the actual direction of the new poems, they confirm one's impressions of the travel-poems, and of the poet in those poems. The image is that of the seeker. For all their flexibility, many of the earlier poems suggested fixed perspectives; it was a poetry of metaphor, "conceits," allegories, pastoral worlds from which the speakers saw men at a distance; and also a poetry of urgent but impersonal tones. This kind of poetry still persists, but rather than move within the frames of metaphor, many of the travel-poems lead outward; in them, "nature" (with the rather fixed attitudes earlier implied in that term) becomes "experience." The speakers in the travel-poems come to accept their personalities; and yet they seek myth in their present circumstances. They are content to be human.

NOTES

INTRODUCTION

[1] Earle Birney, [Reply to R. L. McDougall's essay "The Dodo and the Cruising Auk: Class in Canadian Literature," *Canadian Literature*, No. 18 (Autumn, 1963), 6-20]

[2] *Ibid.*, 77-78. For a description of his early education and jobs, see Birney's "On Being a Canadian Author," *Canadian Library Association Bulletin*, IX (November, 1952), 77-79.

[3] *Canadian Literature*, No. 20 (Spring, 1964), 78.

[4] [Letter to the Editor] *Northern Review*, IV (June-July, 1951), 48.

[5] See Earle Birney, "Canada Calling, Part I," *The Canadian Forum*, 26 (May, 1946), 31-32; "Part II," 26 (June, 1946), 59-61.

[6] See Earle Birney, "Extracts from a letter to Mr. Philip Child, Bursar of the Canadian Author's Association, in resigning from the Association, 15 November, 1948," in *The Making of Modern Poetry in Canada*, edited by Louis Dudek and Michael Gnarowski (Toronto: Ryerson, 1967), pp. 147-148.

[7] Between July 25 and October 24, 1953, *Saturday Night* published six articles by Birney about life in France.

[8] In 1955 – in the issues of August 20, October 15, and November 12 – *Saturday Night* published three articles by Birney about life in Mexico.

[9] Birney has written a few biographical essays on Lowry, and has (with the assistance of Mrs. Lowry) compiled bibliographies of Lowry's writings.

CHAPTER 1

[10] "SP" refers to *Selected Poems, 1940-1966* (Toronto: McClelland and Stewart, 1966). In my text, I shall often abbreviate the titles of Birney's volumes, and put page references within parentheses.

[11] In his notes in *Twentieth Century Canadian Poetry* (Toronto: Ryerson, 1953), Birney says that "The metre is a five-beat line with a varying number of unaccented syllables" (p. 147). This comment suggests that Birney is working within the Anglo-Saxon strong-stress tradition, in which only the primary stresses really matter. (I shall have more to say later about Birney's use of this prosodic system.) In the present case, it is more useful, it seems to me, to account for a "foot-prosody" which emphasizes the iambic-anapestic metre of "David."

[12] Birney writes: "Most lines are 'run-on'; i.e. the sense flows over without breath pause; the purpose is to maintain a sense of narrative movement..." (*Twentieth Century Canadian Poetry*, p. 147).

[13] If I'd been just a little more interested in trying to make the two characters in ["David"]more complex and realistic, I'd have tried it as a

short story. But I wanted to present, as intensely as I could, the symbolic aspect of my two characters, in relation to certain values of life and death, and to the conflicts between man and nature, and between loyalty and guilt in man":*The Creative Writer* (Toronto: CBC Publications, 1966), p. 39.

[14]In his chapter on Birney, Desmond Pacey quotes from a letter in which Birney describes the origins of "David": see Pacey's *Ten Canadian Poets* (Toronto: Ryerson, 1958), pp. 305-306. For a good analysis of "David", see Roy Daniells, "Earle Birney et Robert Finch," *Gants du Ciel*, 11 (printemps, 1946), 85-90.

CHAPTER 2

[15]*Ten Canadian Poets*, p. 307.
[16]*David and other Poems* (Toronto: Ryerson, 1942), p. 22. For permission to quote this poem, as well as other lines from this volume, I thank Mr. Birney.

CHAPTER 3

[17]In a review of *David and Other Poems*, Northrop Frye, writing about Birney's Anglo-Saxon poems, asserted that the technique "easily gets out of hand. It does so, for instance, when the alliteration becomes part of an over-elaborate pattern of repetition – the rhymes, for example, are sometimes harsh and insensitive – and it does so when the use of kennings and compound words makes the diction sound rather spiky and self-conscious": *The Canadian Forum*, XXII (December, 1942), 279. Maybe so, but the fact is that we have no real criteria for the modern poem which uses the prosody of the Anglo-Saxons. We need something more than Frye's affective criticism.

CHAPTER 4

[18]*Now Is Time* (Toronto: Ryerson, 1945), p.6. My thanks to Mr. Birney for permission to quote.

CHAPTER 5

[19]*The Strait of Anian* (Toronto: Ryerson, 1948), pp. 82 and 83. My thanks to Mr. Birney for permission to quote these and other lines from this volume.
[20]*Ibid.*, p.78.
[21]*Ibid.*, p. 80.
[22]"La tradition Narrative dans la Poésie Canadienne-Anglaise," *Gants du Ciel*, 11 (printemps),20.

CHAPTER 6

[23]Desmond Pacey offers the notion that Birney is a "chronicler" of his time. See Pacey's book *Ten Canadian Poets*, pp. 293-294.
[24]*Twentieth Century Canadian Poetry*, p. 150.

CHAPTER 7

[25]"A Unified Personality: Birney's Poems," *Canadian Literature*, No. 30 (Autumn, 1966), 9.
[26]"Up, Over, and Out," *Tamarack Review*, 42 (Winter, 1967), 65, 66.
[27]"Earle Birney and the Compound Ghost," *Canadian Literature*, No. 13 (Summer, 1962), 9.

SELECTED BIBLIOGRAPHY

The Rare Book Room of the University of Toronto Library has the nearest thing to a complete collection of books, manuscripts, and papers; with a card catalogue.

A recent complete bibliography by Peter C. Noel-Bentley and Earle Birney appears in the *West Coast Review*, 5, No. 1 (Spring-Summer, 1970), 86-89.

Books (listed chronologically)

David and Other Poems. Toronto: Ryerson, 1942

Now Is Time: Toronto: Ryerson, 1945.

The Strait of Anian. Toronto: Ryerson, 1948.

Turvey: A Military Picaresque. Toronto: McClelland and Stewart, 1949. Paperback reprint, with an introduction by George Woodcock: McClelland and Stewart, New Canadian Library, 1963.

Trial of a City and Other Verse. Toronto: Ryerson, 1952.

Twentieth Century Canadian Poetry, edited by Earle Birney. Toronto: Ryerson, 1953.

Down the Long Table. Toronto: McClelland and Stewart, 1955.

Ice Cod Bell or Stone. Toronto: McClelland and Stewart, 1962.

Selected Poems of Malcolm Lowry, edited, with the assistance of Margerie Lowry, and with an introduction by Earle Birney. San Francisco: City Lights Books, 1962.

Near False Creek Mouth. Toronto: McClelland and Stewart, 1964.

The Creative Writer. Toronto: Canadian Broadcasting Corporation, CBC Publications, 1966.

Selected Poems, 1940-1966. Toronto: McClelland and Stewart, 1966.

Memory No Servant. Trumansburg, N.Y.: New Books, 1968.

The Poems of Earle Birney. New Canadian Library selection, with an introduction by the author. Toronto: McClelland and Stewart, 1969.

Pnomes, Jukollages, and Other Stunzas. Toronto: Ganglia Press, 1969 (*Gronk*, Ser. 4, No. 3).

Rag and Bone Shop. Toronto: McClelland and Stewart, 1971.

Essays, Articles and Short Stories (listed chronologically)

"Proletarian Literature: Theory and Practice," *The Canadian Forum*, 17 (May, 1937), 58-60.

"Two William Faulkners," *The Canadian Forum*, 18 (June, 1938), 84 et seg.

"The Fiction of James T. Farrell," *The Canadian Forum*, 19 (April, 1939), 21-24.

"To Arms with Canadian Poetry," *The Canadian Forum*, 19 (January, 1940), 322-324.

"Canadian Poem of the Year: *Brébeuf and His Brethren*," *The Canadian Forum*, 20 (September, 1940), 180-181.

"New Verse," *The Canadian Forum*, 20 (October, 1940), 221.

"Sherwood Anderson: A Memory," *The Canadian Forum*, 21 (1941), 82-83.

"Decorated with Anarchisms," *Saturday Night*, 56 (April 12, 1941), 33.

"War and the English Intellectuals," *The Canadian Forum*, 21 (July, 1941), 110-114.

"Advice to Anthologists: Some Rude Reflections on Canadian Verse," *The Canadian Forum*, 21 (February, 1942), 338-340.

"Has Poetry a Future in Canada?" *Manitoba Arts Review*, 5 (Spring, 1946), 7-15.

"Poetry is an Oral Art," *Toronto Globe and Mail*, 22 (June, 1946), 9.

"Extracts from a letter to Mr. Philip Child, Bursar of the Canadian Authors' Association, in resigning from the Association, 15 November, 1948," in *The Making of Modern Poetry in Canada*, edited by Louis Dudek and Michael Gnarowski. Toronto: Ryerson, 1967, 147-148. (Published as "Letter of Resignation from the Editorship of *Canadian Poetry Magazine*," *Here and Now*, I, No. 3 [January, 1949].)

[Letter to the Editor] *Northern Review*, 4 (June-July, 1951), 48.

"On Being a Canadian Author," *Canadian Library Association Bulletin*, 9 (November, 1952), 77-79.

"Enigma in Ebony," (Story) *MacLean's* (October 15, 1953), 16-17, 104, 106-8.

"Cockles, Menhirs, and Café-Exprès, (Travel) "*Saturday Night*, 69 (October 24, 1953), 8.

"The Writer and the H-Bomb," *Queen's Quarterly*, 62 (Spring, 1955), 37-44.

"Mexico without Acapulco," (Travel) *Saturday Night*, 70 (November 12, 1955).

"BC Centennial," *The Canadian Forum*, 38 (April, 1958), 6-8.

"E. J. Pratt and His Critics," in *Our Living Tradition*, Second and Third Series, edited by Robert MacDougall. Toronto: Published in Association with Carleton University by the University of Toronto Press, 1959, pp. 123-147.

"On the Pressing of Maple Leaves," *Canadian Literature*, 6 (1960), 53-56.

"Structural Irony within the 'Summoner's Tale'," *Anglia* (Germany), 78 (1960), 204-218.

[Reply to R. L. McDougall's essay "The Dodo and the Cruising Auk: Class in Canadian Literature," *Canadian Literature*, 18 (Autumn, 1963), 6-20] *Canadian Literature*, 20 (Spring, 1964), 77-80.

[Letter to the Editor] *Tamarack Review*, 30 (Winter, 1964), 96.

"*Turvey* and the Critics," *Canadian Literature*, No. 30 (Autumn, 1966), 21-15.

"Turvey and the Critics," *Canadian Literature*, 30 (Autumn, 1966), 21-15.

"The Canadian Writer versus the Canadian Education," *Evidence*, 10 (1967), 97-113.

"The Many Faces of Vancouver," *Century 1867/1967* (February, 1967), 44-45.

Recordings

David. 45 rp.m. disc (QC-86), 15 mins., read by Earle Birney. Vancouver: Photofolios, 1964. (Available from the author c/o McClelland and Stewart Ltd., 25 Hollinger Rd., Toronto 374).

Canadian Poets on Tape: Birney/Layton. 1 hour cassette tape, ½ hour of each poet. Toronto: Ontario Institute for Studies in Education, 1971.

Earle Birney reads his poems on a 1 hour cassette tape. Toronto: High Barnet, 1970.

Essays, Articles, and Reviews of the Poetry (listed alphabetically)

Bailey, A. G. [Review-article on *The Strait of Anian*] *Dalhousie Review*, 30 (July, 1950), 205-208.

Burns, Gerald. [Review of *Memory No Servant*] *Southwest Review*, 54, No. 1 (Winter 1969), 95.

Carruth, Hayden. "Up, Over and Out," *Tamarack Review*, 42 (Winter, 1967), 61-69.

Colombo, J. R. "Poetic Ambassador" [a review article on *Near False Creek Mouth*], *Canadian Literature*, 24 (Spring, 1965), 55-59.

Congdon, Kirby. [Review of *Selected Poems, 1940-1966*] *Evidence*, 10 (1967), 172-174.

Daniells, Roy. "Earle Birney et Robert Finch," translated into French by Alfred Glauser, *Gants du Ciel*, 11 (printemps, 1946), 83-96.

Crawley, Alan. [Review of *Trial of a City*] *Contemporary Verse*, 39 (1952), 24-25.

Dickson, Robert. [Review of *Rag and Bone Shop*] *Le Soliel* (January 9, 1971).

Drake, Albert. [Review of *Memory No Servant*] *Western Humanities Review*, 23 (Spring, 1969), 179-180.

Elliott, Brian. "Earle Birney: Canadian Poet," *Meanjin* (Australia), 78 (1959), 338-347.

Fredeman, W. E. "Earle Birney: Poet," *British Columbia Library Quarterly*, 23 (1960), 8-15.

Frye, Northrop. [Review of *David and Other Poems*] *The Canadian Forum*, 22 (December, 1942), 278-279.

———. "Canada and Its Poetry," reprinted in *The Making of Modern Poetry in Canada*, edited by Louis Dudek and Michael Gnarowski. Toronto: Ryerson, 1967, 86-97. (The essay had appeared in *The Canadian Forum*, December, 1943).

———. "La Tradition Narrative dans la Poésie Canadienne-Anglaise," *Gants du Ciel*, 11 (printemps, 1946), 19-30. (Although this essay does not mention Birney, it is relevant to his poetry.)

Hollo, Anselm. [Review of *Near False Creek Mouth*] *Ambit* (London), 24 (1965), 41-44.

Holmes, Theodore. [Review of *Selected Poems, 1940-1966*] *Dalhousie Review*, 47, No. 2.

Kearns, Lionel and Copithorne, Judith. [*Review of Rag and Bone Shop*] *Georgia Straight* (Vancouver) (March 3-10, 1971), 21.

Marshall, Tom. [Essay on Birney's Work] Queen's Quarterly (Winter, 1966).

Murphy, R. ed. *Contemporary Poets of the English Language*. Chicago: St. James Press, 1970.

Nesbitt, Bruce [Essay on Birney's Work] *Poetry Australia*, No. 14 (February, 1967), 37-41.

Noel-Bentley, Peter C. "A Study of the Poetry of Earle Birney," M.A., University of Toronto, 1966.

——— and Birney, Earle. [A Birney Bibliography] *West Coast Review*, 5 No. 1 (Spring-Summer, 1970), 86-89.

O'Broin, Padraig. [Review of *Near False Creek Mouth*] *Canadian Poetry* (February, 1965).

Pacey, Desmond. *Creative Writing in Canada*. Toronto: Ryerson, 1952, revised 1961, 150-153.

Purdy, A. W. [Letter to the Editor re Hayden Carruth's review] *Tamarack Review*, 43 (Spring, 1967).

———. [Review of *The Creative Writer*] *Canadian Literature*, 31 (Winter, 1967), 61-64.

———. [Review of *Near False Creek Mouth*] *Fiddlehead*, 65 (1965), 75-76.

Rosenblatt, Joe. [Letter to the Editor re Hayden Carruth's review] *Tamarack Review*, 43 (Spring, 1967).

Rowland, Beryl ed. *Companion to Chaucer Studies* Toronto: Oxford University Press, 1968, 11, 257, 266, 291-305, passim. (Critique of Earle Birney's Chaucerian research.)

Scott, Peter Dale. [Review of *Memory No Servant*] *Poetry* (Chicago) (February, 1970), 353-4.

Shuttle, Penelope. [Review of *Near False Creek Mouth*] *Aylesford Review* (Kent, England), 7 (Winter, 1965), 260-261.

Skelton, Robin. "Canadian Poetry?" *Tamarack Review*, 29 (Autumn, 1963), 71-73.

Smith, A. J. M. "A Unified Personality: Birney's Poems," *Canadian Literature*, 30 (Autumn, 1966), 4-13. (That issue of *Canadian Literature* is offered as "A Salute to Earle Birney.")

Stafford, Wm. [Preface to *Memory No Servant*] Trumansburg, N.Y.: New Books, 1968.

Stainsby, Donald. [Review of *Pnomes, Jukollages, and Other Stunzas*] *Vancouver Sun* (November 20, 1970).

Stevens, Peter. [Review of *Rag and Bone Shop*] *Toronto Globe and Mail* (January 23, 1971).

Weaver, Robert. [Review of *Rag and Bone Shop*] *Toronto Daily Star* (January 30, 1971).

Weatherhead, A. Kingsley. [Review of *Near False Creek Mouth*] *Northwest Review*, 7, No. 1 (Spring-Summer 1965), 86-89.

West, Paul. "Earle Birney and the Compound Ghost," *Canadian Literature*, 13 (Summer, 1962), 5-14.

Wilson, Milton. [Review of *Ice Cod Bell or Stone*] *University of Toronto Quarterly*, 32 (1962-1963), 368-371.

_____. [Review of *Near False Creek Mouth*] *University of Toronto Quarterly*, 34 (1964-1965), 349-351.

_____. "Poet Without a Muse," *Canadian Literature*, 30 (Autumn, 1966), 14-20.

Woodcock, George. [Review of *Selected Poems, 1940-1966*] *The Canadian Forum*, 46 (1966), 115-116.